D1521435

Migration and Politics

Thad A. Brown

Migration and

Politics

The Impact of
Population Mobility on
American Voting Behavior

The University of North Carolina Press

Chapel Hill and London

Library of Congress Cataloging-in-Publication Data

Brown, Thad A.
  Migration and politics.

  Bibliography: p.
  Includes index.
  1. Immigrants—Political activity. 2. Political
participation. 3. Emigration and immigration
—Political aspects. I. Title.
JV6255.B76   1988   323.3′2   87-16240
ISBN 0-8078-1765-1

The paper in this book meets the guidelines for
permanence and durability of the Committee on
Production Guidelines for Book Longevity of the
Council on Library Resources.

92 91 90 89 88   5 4 3 2 1

Design by Kaelin Chappell

For Margaret

Contents

Tables and Figures

Tables

Figures

Acknowledgments

The intellectual roots of this research reach back to when migration was first linked to political behavior by Warren E. Miller in his chapter on population movement in *The American Voter* (Campbell et al. 1960). His article on "one-party politics" showed the importance of lopsided local political environments to individual behavior (Miller 1956). Jacek Kugler insisted that migrants had to change politically. Samuel J. Eldersveld suggested estimating past and current political environments as a way of discovering the effects of migration on citizens. John Sprague and William M. McPhee did pioneering theoretical work on social and contextual effects that informed the spirit of the analysis.

I would like to thank Judith Blake, Ivor Crew, Sam Kernell, Kathleen Knight, Vivian Lew, Dwaine Marvick, John R. Petrocik, Judith L. Powers, Allen A. Russell, David O. Sears, Elizabeth Stephenson, Morry Tolmach, and Donald J. Treiman. Each gave very useful advice and continued support. My colleagues at the University of Missouri-Columbia deserve a special note of thanks for their kindness and generosity.

I would also like to thank Karen Baum, Robert Hardy, Megan Hays, Elizabeth H. Hazard, Paul Hoffman, Charles Hofacker, Shirley Nordhaus, Mette Wadleigh, and Mel Widawski, for their assistance.

Lewis Bateman of the University of North Carolina Press provided the carrot and the stick. Stephanie Sugioka copyedited the manuscript with great care, and Sandra Eisdorfer provided excellent editorial advice.

Introduction

Attempts to understand migration have often relied upon reconstructing the past with the stories of those who moved and the nature of the times in which they lived. And while this book is aimed at objectively re-creating the experiences of migrants and their environments, and in assessing the political consequences of population movement, it is useful to keep in mind the human drama of migration.

Like most, my family migrated. When he was young, my father's family moved from Ballinger, Texas, to Arkansas and Louisiana and back to Texas so many times that half his six brothers and sisters were born in different states. My mother was born in New York of immigrant parents. Toward the end of World War II, she was living in Alabama, working in a town hospital. She never much liked the South, its climate or its ways. After marrying in Alabama, my parents returned to New York to find work and to begin a new life. And in the early 1950s they moved to California to work and to be near family. My father never adjusted to cities and forever wanted to return to the South, to Texas. He never made it back.

Tracking the movement of just my mother's side of the family gives a typical portrait of migration. My mother's brother was the first to move West. He left New York to attend a university in Colorado. He married a young woman from the West and found his first job in the growing aircraft industry in Los Angeles. After my mother joined her brother, my grandparents also left New York for California to begin semiretirement and to be close to their children, grandchildren, and friends.

At one point, nearly a dozen relatives and close friends of my family moved to California from other parts of the country. Among them were my mother's friends and their families from the 600 block of North Sixth Avenue in Mount Vernon, New York. Many of my mother's generation had attended Our Lady of Victory Catholic Church. The neighborhood in New York was at least two generations old. It was Irish and Italian. By the time of my mother's generation, the closeness of the families in the neighborhood had blurred kinship lines. An example makes this point. Two brothers were once orphaned at an early age. They were not sent to live with distant relatives nor made wards of the state. Both boys were taken into the homes of families in the neighborhood to be raised as their own. They could not do less. Many in the neighborhood had been raised by friends of their deceased families.

In California, most who migrated have prospered. They are lawyers and engineers and other professionals. But at the end of three decades, they do not see each other very often. They have new old friends. They live in different parts of Los Angeles, but it might as well be different parts of the country. From my mother's generation a few have returned to New York. Several got divorced. None of the children of my generation knows the others well, nor cares to.

I recently returned to the neighborhood in New York that my family left over thirty years ago. Many friends and relatives of my mother's generation are still there. They are close to one another. Their children are friends, and many have married and stayed within the neighborhood or close by. Family seems very important. Their religion seems very important. Their ethnicity seems important.

On the streets around Mount Vernon there were signs of a coming election. The Democrats run the place. Italians seem to be the dominant group within the party. Signs to support one candidate or another were stuck in lawns in front of many houses, placed in shops and stores, and nailed to telephone poles. There was also an Italian community center in the neighborhood that seemed to have an active role in the election.

To me those who migrated are very different from those who stayed—not only in where they live but in how they live. They hold different values, and different too are their hopes for the future and their ties to the past.

In my family those who moved to California are not rugged individualists, extremists, or ideologues. They also are not loyal Democratic partisans, nor are they active in Italian community organizations. Their politics, much like their religion and other group attachments and loyalties, have been shaped by their personal experiences in California. Their jobs, their new neighborhoods, their community, and their friends have forged new lasting political orientations that are rooted in different political values than are found in Mount Vernon.

Their move West represents a typical form of chain migration, individuals moving to be near kin and family. Yet individual members had to live and to work on a day-to-day basis apart from their traditional support groups. As a consequence, the family, the glue that binds individuals to the politics they inherit, has been eroded by changed circumstances. In the West social group ties changed, and with them the political behavior of my family changed from the way it would have been had they not moved.

Each one who leaves home and moves far away begins a new life. The accounts of migrants and their experiences, unlike the biographies of great political leaders or accounts of major political events, are about how everyday life has changed from the way it was elsewhere. Those stories, if they are truthfully told, might reveal the devastating human costs in terms of the pain and the terror of migration. They also might include the rags-to-riches dreams that come true. I doubt if this is too different today than it was when the country was new and the frontier was the last place settled.

Understanding migration's consequences was once only possible by going through the chronicles of the time. What do they tell us? The most reliable evidence is about the actual process of migrating, the move itself. Not too long ago, the journey to the new place often occurred in the most hostile and violent environments. There is the story of the blacksmith who walked from Rhode Island to New York in midwinter with his wife and children. What attracted them and others were the stories they had heard of fortunes and opportunities for a new life (Birkbeck 1818). Repeatedly the main motive remained the personal, social, and economic gains from migration (Smith 1980:chap. 44).

Often, historical efforts at systematic research on migration have been simple descriptive accounts and limited ad hoc analyses amounting to little more than stories concocted about types of migrants or migration streams. With newspaper accounts, journals of foreign visitors, and memoirs of contemporaries, popular writers and scholars have tried to piece together, in the absence of theory, the life experiences of early American migrants. Hence, movement into the Piedmont during the 1760s to 1780s, when not described in terms of soil and climate conditions, was discussed in terms of the language and social and religious differences among German and Scotch-Irish immigrants of the interior region and the aristocratic planters of the Tidewater (Alvord 1912; Knittle 1936; Ford 1915). Or,

as in the case of the Lake Plains and the Prairies, attention was focused on the events surrounding the removal of Indian tribes and
the availability of easy entry via the Erie Canal (Prucha 1953; Pooley
1908; Cole 1938). Whether involving population streams moving in
the early 1800s into the Allegheny Plateau or across the Mississippi
Valley and the Far West frontiers, the nature of most inquiries has
been atheoretical and ultimately insignificant in its contribution to
our understanding of the relation of human migration to human
behavior.

I became interested in the political effects of migration after visit-
ing my family in New York and reflecting on the striking differences
between New York (nonmigrant) and California (migrant) family
members. I did not think that there could be important differences
between the kinds of people who migrated and those who did not
migrate, but the differences in their political attitudes and behavior
were striking. Is it possible that migration caused political differences
in individuals? Is it possible that individual people with almost identical characteristics (family socialization, income, education, ethnicity, occupational status, religion, and community and peer background) could as adults adopt different political attitudes and
behaviors because of different environments? Is it the environment
which causes political behavior? My training as a political scientist
told me that this could not be true, but there it was. That same
training demanded that I devise hypotheses which could be falsified
(that is, statements which could be proven to be false if they were
false) by empirical means rather than casual observation, anecdote,
and reflection. This book is a report of my investigation of the effect
of migration on politics.

An Overview

I have divided this book into three parts. Part I concentrates on
the migrant. In Chapter 1 I set out competing theories of political
migration. Chapter 2 describes the social, economic and political attributes and attitudes of migrants in general and classifies by type of
migration experience. The potential that the migration experience
per se has for influencing micropolitical behavior is also set forth.
Chapter 3 focuses on the political attributes of those who have been
involved in major streams of regional movement. Migration to the
Far West, the South-North population exchange, and the movement
between urban and rural places are important parts of the American
migratory story. Migrants within each stream are described in terms

of their political attributes both at the times of migration and later on. The macro effects of internal migration are also assessed. Thus Part I describes the distinctive characteristics of migrants in the United States and the nearly permanent geographic streams that define the contours of American migration.

Part II deals with the consequences of either staying within or changing political environments. These chapters show how changing political environments can determine, reinforce, or alter micropolitical attributes. Chapter 4 defines the measures and methods used to study the consequences of changing political environments. The meaning of political context is defined. In Chapter 5, I show how migrants who cross political environmental boundaries compare to those who do not. The chapter focuses primarily on the migrant's voting behavior and party identification. It treats a migrant's adaptation to new political environments as a function of previous and current contextual experiences. Factors which should diminish the effects of external political environments, early socialization and political information, are shown in Chapter 6 to play an unexpected role in forming a migrant's response to contextual change.

Part III considers further political consequences of migration. Chapter 7 argues that migrants who change contexts rely on objective self-interest considerations for voting decisions. It is suggested that losing partisan loyalties through migration results in the development of self-styled personalized political beliefs.

And finally Chapter 8 summarizes the findings of this book, and draws together the aggregate and contextual analysis presented earlier. It questions the traditional theory which suggests that migration as a social phenomenon does not have a role to play in forging the political behavior and attitudes of individual migrants. As a social mechanism that weakens the attachment of individuals to their groups, migration appears to provide the opportunity of flushing out diseconomies associated with entrenched group interests. As a theoretical ending point, migration may give us further insight into the primacy of group versus individual orientations to politics. As a consequence, internal migration may be an ongoing mechanism that plays a sub rosa role in national or regional politics.

Part I

Political Migrants

Chapter 1

A Theory of
Political Migration

Three moves are equal to one fire.

—Benjamin Franklin, *Poor Richard's Almanac*

Hamelin Pool is an inlet off of Sharks Bay on the northwest coast of Australia. The flow of water from the bay is blocked at its entrance by a natural sandbar on which grows eel grass. That combined with the intense heat of the tropical sun causes the water of the tidal pool to be extremely salty and consequently inhospitable to most sea creatures. Blue-green algae, a distant relative of the green algae found today in backyard pools and in low-rent apartments, grows wherever there is sufficient moisture. It is a primitive life form, one of the first complex ensembles of cells to be able to feed off its environment by extracting hydrogen from water. Algae grows to unusual size in Hamelin Pool because predators such as mollusks cannot live in the salty waters. Because the physical environment in which it lives has not changed, the blue-green algae exists, some naturalists believe, as it did when it was the most advanced form of life two billion years ago (Attenborough 1980). Elsewhere, as at Gunflint Chert on Lake Superior, only its fossils remain in strange, round shapes that today are no more than stains on rocks at the lake's edge.

Evolution only occurs when environments change. In many ways man has escaped the dictates of environment. Through accumulated collective wisdom, the consequences of pitiless shifts in the physical environment can be thwarted, most of the time at least. Yet social environments within which man lives are not under control. Life is still adapting to the effects of changing human environments.

In this book I examine the political consequences of geographical mobility for citizens in the United States. I show that internal migration has pronounced effects on citizens' political actions and loyalties and beliefs. The effect is not the product of the social, economic, or political composition of migrants; nor is it a result of the easily recognized characteristics of population movement streams (north-to-south, east-to-west, rural-to-urban) considered to be politically important. The political effects of migration instead result from individuals who adapt to local political environments. As the following chapters show, migrants play a game with nature as they move from one local political environment to another. Sometimes migrants change political environments; sometimes not. When migrants change political environments, as we will see, the change of environments changes their political attributes permanently. Their voting behavior adapts over time to match the dominant political party of their new local political environment. Migrants who change political environments, however, fail to develop clear psychological commitments to political parties, and end up thinking of themselves as political independents. This seeming contradiction of adapting political behavior completely while unraveling partisan identification appears to be rooted in the cause of migrants' political behavior. The political behavior of migrants who change political environments becomes less a function of traditional, social group partisanship and more the product of objective, personal experiences. Migrants' political actions are mediated by early learned political norms and values less than would be expected based on previous research on voting behavior. A migrant who changes political environments votes with a greater reliance on personal self-interest and finally holds what appear to be individualized preferences on issues of public policy. Thus political change occurs not only by the planned actions of governments or the behavior of elites, but also by the actions of ordinary people who migrate.

Internal Migration

Migration is usually described in geographical or economic terms. The theoretical controversies in the literature focus on who migrates and why (Brown and Neuberger 1977; Greenwood 1975). Rarely are migrations within a country studied for their social, psychological, or political consequences. This is in sharp contrast to the volumes written on the human consequences of immigration, migration into a new country. Foreign immigration is considered a dramatic and colorful story of human conflict and change. Compared to the image that eighteenth or nineteenth century immigration evokes, the businessman moving from Greenwich to Dallas is not very exciting. The difference, which I believe has been overdrawn, rests on the assumptions made about geographical mobility.

The study of immigration has centered on if or when ethnics and immigrants blend into a new culture. The process that assimilates nationalities is long and brutal. It estranges family members of different generations. It induces group conflict between newer and older immigrants. It forges from the cultural roots of competing social groups the major blocs of political cleavage (Lipset and Rokkan 1967:chap. 1; Hays 1957:chaps. 2, 4). Thus immigration is viewed as an important phenomenon for both the individual and society.

How does internal migration, the movement within a country, compare to immigration from a different country? Some internal migration results from purely economic motives. Most often people move within a country to find better jobs and economic opportunities. The reasons can range from a job transfer to the changing importance of industrial sectors which changes aggregate labor demands. People also migrate for personal and social reasons—to leave home or to return home. Going to college, reuniting a family, breaking up a family, finding a comfortable retirement area are also important causes of migration.

Migration is assumed to leave the individual better off economically and socially. Whatever the ambivalence the migrant might have at the time he or she moves, the assumption is that the migration leads to occupational success, greater educational attainment, and increased income—leaving the mobile population better off than the nonmovers (Blau and Duncan 1967).

Advanced industrial economies are considered to be able to sustain their development and growth only with internal migration. For American society and economy, a fluid labor force is assumed to be a major source of economic benefit. Citizens without jobs are encouraged to migrate to places where jobs exist and to seek their own prosperity. Communities strapped by economic decline are then saved the cost of supporting the unemployed and their families with expensive social welfare programs.

Neither migrants nor society, however, reap only benefits from migration. Internal migration often induces many of the problems of culture shock, uprooting, and assimilation that are experienced through immigration. Moreover, communities or states that lose population often lose their most employable workers. The area as a consequence loses its long-term self-sustaining capability.

The distinction between the consequences of foreign immigration and internal migration has been overstated. Geographical mobility redefines associations, friendships, neighborhood, and community. The migrant may find that geographical dislocations force contacts with people whose norms, values, and beliefs differ greatly from anything familiar. Migration can break down traditions and customs and hence free individuals from old forms of social dependence. Being free from old ties may provide individuals with new avenues of opportunity and personal development. But breaking these ties may also induce misery, discontent, and alienation as a result of the personal isolation and uprooting which accompany leaving home.

Change comes from a variety of sources besides migration. People and societies are changed by wars, natural disasters, and technological or industrial innovations (Mendras 1967). Change can also emanate from the individual. Social and economic mobility allows levels of achievement which may surpass those of previous generations. Or when youthful dreams are not reached, they may be brought into line with adult reality as a person lowers future expectations. Often, however, these sources of personal change precede or follow migration. For many, a migration remains an important life event. It draws into focus the future; at times it destroys continuity with the past.

Theories of adaptation and assimilation and integration have at their heart a view that the natural condition of man is sedentary. People belong somewhere. They should be members of some community, inheriting and passing on the norms and values of their past and place of origin. Those who move, and this is especially true of immigrants from foreign countries, are often considered different not only because they are from a foreign culture, or speak a different language or speak with an accent, but because they have left their home, family, and community behind for a new place.

American society thus presents a paradox. It is the norm to move. Statistically, every year nearly 20 percent of the population change residences. Within this group, around 7 percent migrate within their own state but across a county boundary, 3.5 percent migrate within their own region, and 2.5 percent migrate across regions. Over the course of their lives, 75 percent of the American population migrate at least once, and many migrate more than once. The amount of contemporary migration produces enough movement to actually "depopulate within five years, all 223 current U.S. metropolitan areas with under one million residents" (Morrison and Wheeler

1978:77). Most places do not empty, of course, because inmigration tends to balance out outmigration.

Migration within the United States is in stark contrast to other countries, advanced or not. Germans, Italians, French, and English in comparison to Americans rarely leave the communities of their origin. In terms of migration, even rapidly developing societies in the third world where the bulk of the population movement is between urban and rural places still pale by comparison to the United States (Jackson 1969; Brown and Neuberger 1977; Thomas and Hunter 1977; von Kaufmann 1975; Zachariah and Conde 1981). How is this demographic phenomenon related to politics?

Political Migration

Migration physically separates the familiar and the new. By migrating, a person may end up in social settings and among new groups where earlier learned norms and customary behavior are judged wrong or inappropriate or where only certain types of action and specific beliefs are given positive reinforcement. The link between migration and politics is based on the effect that changing social and political environments have on an individual's political attitudes and behavior. Migration provides a unique way in which individuals can change their local political environments.

Early social scientists looked at the individual effect of local environments. Rousseau's concept of the general will, Tonnies's argument that community superseded blood ties in the determination of individual roles and relationships, Simmel's investigations into group structure—all represent efforts to discover what Durkheim labeled the conscience collective and how it is related to personal attitudes and behavior.[1]

Overlapping Political Environments

The environment defines types of personal contact or social interaction which can reinforce or break down existing values and patterns of habitual behavior. The composition and size of different groups within an environment give clues to the number and the type of social interactions in a social or community setting.

As early as the 1930s, Herbert Tingsten found that social milieu has clear political consequences. Tingsten (1937) reported that class-based political parties get more votes than they should expect to receive given the distributions of working-class or middle-class members in given areas. His notion that a "center of social gravity" exists reduces to a consideration that people are influenced politically by the social groups around them. Similar findings for social class and other social and political factors were reported by Berelson et al. 1954; McPhee 1963; Miller 1956; Katz and Eldersveld 1961; Valen and Katz 1964.[2]

Environmental forces no doubt overlap and are nested with one another. Some aspects of an environment may be local, that is particular to a given area; others may be national. Some components of an environment may touch the individual with greater frequency or have greater salience. A political environment can influence an individual in many ways. A few of the more obvious examples are informal chats in the family or neighborhood, interaction with work or church groups, face-to-face contacts with campaign workers and elected government officials, or one-way communications from the mass media. The influence of a local political environment hinges on the nature of both the individual and social networks that give to a bounded setting a political coloration.[3]

Investigating the political effects of migration comes close to being an experiment with nature. The nature of the migration governs the degree of the similarity or difference between a new place and a previous one. After migration, the individual confronts a measurably similar or different political environment. If the previous and current political environments are the same, the social interactions which stem from the local political environment should be the same, and the migrant should show no outward signs of a migration. If the two political environments are different, however, the new political environment will present the individual with a different, incongruent set of political cues. Migration presents the potential for change by exposing the individual to a different political environment.

Of minimal importance to a theory of political migration are the limiting, immunizing effects of prior political experiences or early political socialization. Migrants are assumed to depend only on the impetus for change to change their political attributes. In this case the source of change is a complete and instantaneous shift in the partisan nature of the local political environment.

What makes a typical migrant susceptible to a new political environment is not only that he or she is usually young when migrating but also that local political environments can completely change. Most migration occurs between the ages of eighteen and thirty (Lansing and Mueller 1967:39; U.S. Bureau of the Census 1966:18). This is a period of life when a person is recurrently challenged by new friends, co-workers, fellow students, and others in the community on many of the beliefs learned earlier. Breaking family ties and increasing personal independence as the individual begins adulthood can lead to greater dependence on the external milieu than would have existed earlier or later in life (Brim and Wheeler 1966). A relatively constant environment throughout this period of life might enable the individual to thwart pressures for change or to remain impervious to massive personal dislocation. But if former support groups—those that make up the individual's initial political reality—are too distant after migration to counter the pressure for change, different political beliefs and values may emerge. A human environment is a social and political context within which a person lives. In politics, along with the national state of political affairs, an environment is the setting within which political behavior interactions occur. Contexts are composed of friends, a neighborhood, acquaintances and co-workers, voluntary organizations, political parties, and mass media. When concentrated, they form for a citizen a reference point and a social base for political understanding and behavior.

Social environments tend to persist even when an individual appears to change. Going away to college, getting married, or entering the army are not associated with a predictable change in political attributes. A reason commonly given is that few who experience the conditions for change actually alter the social environments in which they live (Middleton and Putney 1963:377–83; Jackman 1972: 462–72). There are many examples of this. Newcomb's study of Bennington College graduates (Newcomb et al. 1967) and the early work of Berelson, Lazarsfeld, and McPhee (1954) showed that once an individual establishes social networks and environments, they remain largely intact throughout life. In instances of social class mobility, such as in Great Britain, Butler and Stokes found that personal contacts with friends and acquaintances and co-workers are often with those from the class of origin (Butler and Stokes 1976). Thus the pressures for change are often an illusion. A person may simply decide, consciously, to retain friends, family, and casual acquaintances irrespective of immediate circumstance. Values shared in common at an early time in life may be powerful human bonds, and sources of continuity and stability.

Yet stable and enduring social and political environments in a highly modern society are increasingly difficult to maintain. The external world constantly intrudes into people's political consciousness. And if group structures and identities are not in place or intact, the potential that the external world has for inducing political change increases.

Alternate Theories

A Socialization Theory

Probably the dominant view up to this time is that in the United States geographic mobility has been found not to change people politically. This conclusion is based on research conducted nearly three decades ago at the University of Michigan. The analysis relied upon examining individual respondents in national surveys who moved within or across regional boundaries or from rural to urban places. Political environments were equated with the political tendencies typical in the South or in the rural Midwest or in the Far West. The theory is that political socialization forms virtually permanent political loyalties that immunize migrants from the force of new political environments, however persuasive those new environments might be.

In a more generalized form, the political socialization theory stresses that when a person is socialized as a political actor, he enters a state of stable equilibrium. That is, if for some reason there is a lapse in his or her normal political behavior—a vote defection induced because of a weak incumbent, a particular issue of importance, or a scandal—because of basic partisan loyalties socialized early on in life, the citizen would eventually return to his party of origin. Persistence means that core values remain steadfast even when the individual behavior wavers, or when there are two objective conditions which should cause change (Sears et al. 1980).

Of course individuals would not be affected by migration if they did not change political environments when moving from place to place. Migrants may, through some self-selection process, remain within the same political environment after migration as before. But many migrants do change their political environment. According to Converse, however, "It has been documented that partisan preferences of individuals do tend to survive change in residence very admirably, even when the voter migrates into strongholds of the opposition" (1966:10). Converse's conclusion rests upon the notion that basic political attributes once learned tend to survive in the face of most situational changes experienced after childhood. Psychological predispositions tend to immunize individual political beliefs and long-term political behavior from the political forces of direct experience, changing milieus, or even catastrophic events.

American migrants' voting behavior, party identification, and electoral participation have been found to remain more or less identical with those of the nonmobile populations in the areas of origin.

White southerners migrating to the West tended to retain the political attitudes and behavioral characteristics typical of the South. In the 1950s, of former southerners living in the West,

> four out of five party identifiers report no change in their party identifications, and their reported Democratic partisanship does not depart substantially from that of Southerners who had not ventured from home. . . . Further . . . their presidential vote in 1952 and 1956 more than reflected the Democratic sentiment of their region of origin. . . . In short, the movement of an extremely Democratic group into a relatively more Republican environment appears to have resulted in virtually no individual change or dilution of Democratic allegiances. (Campbell et al. 1960:448–49)

A nearly identical story holds for other migrant groups. Southern Democrats moving to the Midwest tend to remain Democrats. Northern Republicans relocating in the South and the Border states tend to retain their Republican partisan predispositions. Northern urbanites migrating to more Republican suburbs remain Democrats. Urban voters raised in rural areas of the North—a traditional Republican milieu—stay with their Republican heritage and raise their children as Republicans (Campbell et al. 1960).

But There Are Examples of Political Adaptation

The indigenous population has been found to be influenced by the new political loyalties and values of returning migrants. Dogan suggests that the spread of the Communist party in southern Italy resulted in part from a curious multistep political contagion of rural nonmigrants by the leftist partisanship of returning relatives and friends from the urban, industrial areas. The sons and daughters of villagers of the South, who had migrated to northern Italy, Germany, France, and Switzerland remained voting residents of their original hometown. For election day, they returned home on trips subsidized by the government to see family and friends and to vote. Because of their changed social milieu, many of these ex-ruralites had become supporters or members of the Italian Communist party after they had taken up residence in the industrial centers. The returning migrants converted friends and relatives, and began the process of moving their villages from traditional support of the Italian Right to strong partisanship backing for the parties of the Left (Dogan 1967:189).

In the United States the only example of adaptation after migration is the electoral mobilization of southern blacks who migrated to
the North in the interwar years. The votes and participation of rural
southern blacks were believed to be developed by their migration to
northern urban areas. After migrating, many blacks experienced
their first taste of electoral politics. Most blacks who moved to the
North also developed political values more like the blacks born in the
urban North (Campbell et al. 1960:452).

In the case of both the Italian migrants coming from agricultural
areas in the South and rural southern blacks in the U.S. who migrate
to the North, the explanation for their apparent adaptation to new
social environments is attributed to their having missed early political socialization. Rural Italians were in Dogan's words available voters who came from a segment of the population which traditionally
did not vote. Southern blacks did not develop partisan values
through early political socialization because their parents were re-
stricted by local statutes or custom from registering to vote and participating in elections.

Areas Change Politically

It is important to note that migration includes macropolitical effects whether or not micropolitical change occurs. Political effects
have been linked to the numerical shuffling of population. Reappor-
tionment and redistricting issues and the political composition of
those coming to and leaving major geographical regions have been
linked to net migration. For example, on the basis of population
movement as monitored by the 1980 census, eight seats in the House
of Representatives were lost from the mid-Atlantic states of New
York and Pennsylvania, while Texas's share of the House seats increased by three (Hauser 1981).

What gives further credence to the nonadaptability of migrants is
that a residue of the past migrations often lasts long after the movement stream dries up. Indiana is a state where contemporary regional patterns of partisanship have their roots in the character of the
settlers at the time of the Civil War. Southern counties in Indiana
were traditionally Democratic strongholds mostly because of the
Southern in-migrants. In contrast, in Republican areas such as
Wayne County, the early settlers were Quakers whose abolitionist
attitudes made them early Republican supporters (Key and Munger
1959:283).

A similar tendency was found for the north-to-south migration
stream in the 1950s. Northern middle-class professionals who mi-

grated to the South after World War II were both attracted by and contributed to the economic recovery of the region. These northern-bred Republicans moved in sufficient numbers and retained their earlier partisan loyalties so that they weakened the Democratic dominance of the region. The political composition of the southern population also changed because of the out-migration of southern Democrats. Over a twenty-year period, Converse estimated that the political consequences of the net migration alone were sufficient to reduce the expected proportion voting Democratic in the region .25 percent per year, or 5 percent over the entire period as Republicans replaced Democrats (Converse 1966:230, n. 12).

Problems in Past Assumptions

The simple process of the exchange or the replacement of partisans was the focus of past macropolitical analysis because migrants were not found to adapt politically to places assumed to be different political environments.

Past research further assumed that the persistence of early socialization meant that individuals would remain unaffected by both migration and changed political environments. In adults selective exposure and psychological immunization were considered the prime factors that limited a migrant's response to a changed environment.

Selective exposure takes the form of people's seeking out supportive and familiar information and/or avoiding nonsupportive, nonfamiliar information (Sears 1968). For migration studies, this process has obvious attractions. Many individuals enter a new place already employed or familiar with their jobs, or they are members of professional organizations or social groups or other organizations. Each contact may serve as a source of continuity in a person's life and is often associated with previous acquaintances, family, or friends. Even when such integrative personal relationships are absent, the migrant may still be exposed to a milieu in the new area similar to that found in the old area. A migrant may still listen to or watch the same national news programs, take the same magazines and newspapers, and associate with like-minded persons. When one's past life is re-created in a new place, it means the individual is unwittingly selecting from the environment those social and political cues that will be received. This may occur even when the move is to a very different political environment.

If information is sought or avoided on the basis of whether it supports existing beliefs, there would be no effect on the individual's

political beliefs from entering a new place. If the individual has political beliefs as a result of self-selection, does it matter where he lives
or works, or whether the Democrats or the Republicans have the
most voters in the area, or whether the composition of an area
changes as a result of migration?

The best evidence to date does not warrant expectations that selective exposure occurs. From a multitude of studies—some experimental, others not—individuals do not seem to

> protect their pre-existing attitudes very vigorously by using the
> mechanism of selective exposure. Indeed, there seem to be
> equally numerous cases in which they choose exposure to the op-
> posite point of view. Neither has it been possible to isolate condi-
> tions under which people would be especially likely to use selec-
> tive exposure, although a number have been hypothesized (high
> dissonance, low confidence, difficulty of refutation, high commit-
> ment, etc.). It now seems likely that people simply are not espe-
> cially prone to use selective exposure when they are strongly mo-
> tivated to protect their own options. (Sears 1975)

Therefore migrants across political environments are not likely to
selectively avoid or pay attention to specific political information.

Psychological immunity is a second process commonly associated
with the stability of adult political beliefs and attitudes. Immunity to
a change of political environments is assumed to work much like
biological immunity. Immunity from the influence of new political
information, in spite of direct contact with different types of people
or conflicting media associated with changing political environments
is assumed to result from prior repeated doses of incongruent political information.

For political actions and beliefs, immunity is thought to be developed by repeated exposure to electoral politics, especially exposure
to political information contrary to one's beliefs (McPhee 1963:chap.
2). Resistance to change also appears to be reinforced by action. Voting, working in campaigns, contributing money and other resources,
and repeatedly discussing political issues—these not only indicate a
greater degree of interest in politics but, along with increasing one's
commitment to a political process, harden partisan and ideological
beliefs. More direct experience in politics yields a stronger set of
partisan loyalties from which stems the ability to thwart new political
information.

The absence of immunization is the explanation given for the
micropolitical effects associated with migration. The rapid adaptation

of blacks from the South to the political culture of the urban North is attributed to the blacks' lack of experience in electoral politics prior to their trek to the North from the South (Campbell et al. 1960; Marvick 1965). The same argument is made for migration's effects on rural southern Italians, both those exposed to the northern industrial (leftist) political culture and those of the indigenous population remaining in the South who were affected by the radicalized views of the returning migrants.

Psychological immunity has come to imply that a person is immune to the forces of change. But psychological immunity may be different for people depending upon the sum of their past experiences. As a consequence, their adaptation may take place by a matter of degrees. Consider migrants from solidly Republican environments who move to Democratic strongholds. A highly immunized migrant might be less influenced by a new political environment and thus become only 30 percent Democratic. Over a series of elections he or she may vote for a Democrat more often than before the move but less often than a fully committed Democrat would. A weakly immunized migrant might end up being 60 percent Democratic and a non-immunized person might be 80 percent Democratic, all from the same exposure. Psychological immunity may in turn produce a mixture of partisan responses to comparable environmental forces, but for adaptation to occur, there should be a uniform shift in the migrant's partisan attributes in the direction of the dominant political environment. For some, migration could result in their being mobilized into a partisan camp, whereas for others, the shift in political environments resulting from migration may cause partisan demobilization as a result of gradual movement to nonpartisanship or political independence.[4]

Thus total psychological immunity as a process of blocking micropolitical change associated with migration may have been oversold. Immunity may also emanate from the unnatural stance that approval for one's views is not tied to the present time and place. Immunity in part stems from the ability to seek approval and acceptance from people not immediately present (Brim and Wheeler 1966:17). For those who migrate, resisting the political culture of a new locale may result from the education, status, wealth, or even political experience allowing them to do so. But as I will show, few ever have the resources to remain steadfast on their partisan and political beliefs when everything around them has changed. Remaining impervious to the social pressure to adapt may simply be beyond the capacity of most typical migrants.

Summary

Internal migration is a form of demographic change that may have micropolitical consequences. Migrants may adapt to new political environments and thereby change previous political attitudes, beliefs, and behavior. In some instances, adaptation can mean a complete alteration of an individual's political attributes. Adaptation, however, can also imply a gradual assimilation of behavior and beliefs to a local political culture.

The degree to which a migrant adapts is suspected to be a function of the objective change of political environments, the salience of the current local political environment, and the degree to which experiences have molded a psychological immunity to change. If migrants adapt politically, certain empirical regularities should follow from a change of political environments. Adaptation should be most apparent in those migrants with the weakest political backgrounds and hence the shortest memories of the past. Whether background is measured in terms of political inheritance gained through early political socialization or in terms of political cognitive capacity or political knowledge and interest at the time they make political decisions, those most likely to shift after migration should be those least able to uphold political values of a previous place. This does not include those who consciously reject their past or who anticipate prior to migration the values needed to adapt to a new place.

And finally, the degree to which adaptation occurs should be increased as a function of the partisan homogeneity of the new political environment and the degree to which the new political environment stays the same over time. Current environments which have both homogeneous and stable partisan contours should affect the migrant more than those which are more heterogeneous and changeable in their partisan mixture. Over time, the importance of the previous environment should decline and be replaced by the current political environment.

An openness to change model would dictate a response immediately after a migration. A longer reaction time would indicate something other than persistence of the past but probably not a simple conversion model. The former would be the product of an instantaneous calculus, while the latter would be a result of a breakdown in social, cultural, and economic group norms. Such a breakdown undermines the long-term roots of attitudinal predispositions and the structure of group identification and support.

If citizens change when confronted with the pressure to do so, are they behaving in a thoughtful way or are they merely responding in a mechanical way to external stimuli? Showing that a citizen can change his vote or political attitudes is easy; showing the reasons for the change is not. The conclusion that political change is reasoned change needs proof that the action is related either to newly developed political beliefs, personal experiences, or both, and that they are uniquely related to the migration experience.

Chapter 2

A Description of Migrants

Depend upon it: there is nothing so unnatural as the commonplace.

—Sherlock Holmes, in Arthur Conan Doyle's
The Case of Identity

In this chapter internal migration is formally defined, and migrants are described by measures of socioeconomic status and politics. In this description, migrants are compared with nonmigrants and a cross section of the population. Migrants who were interviewed in 1970 or in 1980 soon after their last move are compared with those who moved earlier. How migrants are different politically given their socioeconomic attributes and the nature of their migration experience (the distance of a move, rural or urban change, and interregional relocation) is considered at the end of the chapter.

Definitions of Migration

Determining and describing who migrates appear to be rather straightforward tasks. A moment's reflection, however, can help illustrate their complexity. The problems concern the definition of migration. Which of the many dimensions of migration should be examined for political consequences? (The data needed to test theoretical propositions are discussed in Appendix A.)

When a move is from the urban Northeast to the rural Southwest, there is little disagreement that the individuals involved are migrants. While migration across regions is important in the shifting political balance between areas of the country, this type of mobility accounts for only a fraction of the yearly residential change in the United States (U.S. Bureau of the Census 1971). To the individual, it is obvious that a move across the country should be more significant than a move down the block. Indeed it is inappropriate to discuss both moves under the same rubric, migration. Yet there seems no straightforward watershed between the act of simply changing residences and migration. A definition must depend on the specific research problem under study.

I use the conventional definition of migration set by the U.S. Bureau of the Census (Shryock 1964:chap. 2). Here, a residential change is classified as a migration whenever the individual crosses a county boundary. Movement of this type customarily places the migrant in a completely different community, making easy personal contact with friends and family from the old community difficult. It forces the migrant to form new relationships, and often coincides with changes in jobs and schools. Crossing a county boundary is also sufficient to bring about a qualitative change in local political environments.

The county unit is the smallest geographic unit in the United States for which systematic historical political information has been gathered. A county has an identifiable political complexion that, we will see, is useful for measuring over a very long period the local political environment.[1] The use of the county in a definition of migration is, of course, not without its drawbacks. Some county boundaries are situated in the middle of expanding urban areas, and may, consequently, result in the incorrect classification of short-hop moves as migrations. The definition may also obscure important community size changes that, while technically not migrations, do bring about important changes in the social setting of the mover. The point remains that most migrations—that is, intercounty moves—are between, not within, urban areas and that most migrants monitored in the national samples used here moved on the average hundreds of miles when they migrated.

A major point of the analysis in this book is that individuals who migrate experience a very slow form of political change. Migration experiences that occur over a lifetime will be useful in showing the effects of slower social and cultural changes associated with migration across regional boundaries or movement from rural or farm areas to more urban places. Such population shifts often take a generation to accomplish and are usually the result of several major migrations. By determining where the respondent lived when young, a comparison can be made between the original state or community setting, providing a valuable insight into regional and community size changes experienced by citizens in the United States through migration. This analysis will be made in Chapter 3.

By isolating the last migration, we can do an analysis of the local political environment to determine the net political impact of a major migration on the individual. Micropolitical effects can be determined by using the last migration experience, the political environmental change experienced when migration occurred, and the political environment at the time of the interview. This analysis will begin in Chapter 4 below.

Socioeconomic Attributes

To proceed with the main task of this book, the analysis of the political consequences of migration, we need a clear understanding of the microsocioeconomic consequences of migration. The massiveness of American migration means that across measures of wealth, status, education, and social and economic mobility, migrants are going to be similar to the total population. In 1980, nearly half of all migrants considered themselves to be members of the middle class. Half had professional or white collar occupations and experienced significant upward mobility from the level of their parents. Around 40 percent of the migrants had a family income of over twenty-five thousand dollars, and 28 percent had one of greater than thirty thousand. Forty percent had attended college. These characteristics correspond almost exactly to the socioeconomic contours of the American population. Isolating just migrants, in fact, is presenting a part-whole artifact in some ways in that the size of internal migration within the United States means that the distribution of all migrants and the total population have to be similar.

Migrants' subjective view of their own economic situation also mirrors that of the total population. When migrants were asked about their personal financial condition compared to a year ago, 43 percent said it was worse, 23 percent said that they were in the same condition, and 33 percent said that they were better off. When they were asked how over the last five years their family's income had changed relative to the cost of living, 31 percent said that their income had stayed even, 14 percent reported an increase, and 55 percent said that they had fallen behind. And when migrants were asked about their financial outlook for the coming year, 32 percent said that they expected to be better off, 47 percent said that they would be in about the same position, and 21 percent believed that they would be economically worse off. These are identical distributions reported for the total population in 1980.

What are the dividends of migration? Migration occurs for a purpose, usually because of expected social and economic benefits for the individual and his or her family. Whether the payoff of migration is considered in terms of real wage increases or less tangible outcomes—such as the potential for greater economic rewards in the future, greater social freedom, or the opportunity for more diverse life experiences—the expectation is that migrants end up better off than those they left behind. The evidence, however, suggests that there are few large socioeconomic dividends associated with migration (Greenwood 1975:412–33). In part the evidence reflects a tendency for past research to focus on the causes of migration rather than its consequences and it's role in redistributing labor resources.

One reason for the meager differences between migrants and the total population may be broad, yet relatively slow shifts in the composition of those migrating in years after they move. At the time of migration, individuals may be a distinctive group. As long-term panel data are not available, comparing migrants at the time they move with migrants later on and with nonmigrants may refine the estimate of the socioeconomic composition and consequences of geographical mobility. Recent migrants can be compared both with nonmigrants as well as with those who migrated at an earlier time. Recent migrants are those whose last migration was within five years. Nonmigrants are those who have lived in the same community all of their life. Comparing recent migrants, migrants within a short time of their latest move, and those for whom the migration experience is more distant can tell us how migration works to self-select certain types of citizens by their social and economic characteristics or change citizens after migration as a result of altered occupational and income mobility or both.

When the most recent migrants are culled from the evidence at hand, and when their attributes are compared to those of earlier migrants, a mixed picture emerges of confounding socioeconomic effects. The evidence from Table 2.1 for example shows curious socioeconomic patterns. On the basis of subjective social class, head of household's occupational status, and respondent's education, those who migrated within five years of 1980 are middle class—more so than earlier migrants, nonmigrants, or even the total population. But for family income and the respondent's objective social mobility based on intergenerational change, the most recent migrants are on the same level as early migrants and the total population.

Most migrants are young. Migration is most likely to take place

Table 2.1. The Comparative Social Base of Migration

	Migrated 1974–1980	Migrated before 1974	Nonmigrants	Total
% Identifying				
Middle Class	53	47	42	47
(N)	(350)	(572)	(337)	(1499)
% Professional or				
White Collar[a]	58	44	47	49
(N)	(272)	(389)	(234)	(1081)
% College				
Educated	50	35	33	37
(N)	(364)	(615)	(346)	(1581)
% High Income[b]	27	29	24	26
(N)	(368)	(617)	(348)	(1336)
% Upwardly Mobile	46	50	41	46
(N)	(242)	(341)	(201)	(1615)
Mean Age	35	49	44	44
(N)	(368)	(617)	(347)	(1612)
	22%	38%	22%	

Source: American National Election Study, 1970; American National Election Study, 1980, Pre and Post Election Surveys, Center for Political Studies, University of Michigan.
[a]Head of household's occupational status.
[b]Family income more than $30,000 before taxes.

either when the individual is very young, between birth and four years old, or in the years after high school, around eighteen through the mid-thirties. There is a small increase in the rate of migration as well after sixty, in the years of retirement (Lansing and Mueller 1967). Age bias has important implications for the socioeconomic description of migrants. As Table 2.1 shows, in 1980 those who migrated within the last five years were drawn heavily from younger cohorts. As a group, younger migrants are not likely to have achieved their full income potential or highest level of occupational status. In the 1980 data, migrants who moved before 1974 have higher income brackets relative to other socioeconomic status measures. This income difference is potentially because they are older than recent migrants. Migration is at times a catalyst to success. At the time of migration, individuals may not have reached the occupational status they eventually will attain. A boost of upward social mobility could be a dividend for many who migrate.

Alternatively recent migrants' higher socioeconomic status could be a product of social mobility which occurred prior to migration. This would mean, of course, that migration self-selects from relatively higher status individuals. Again untying this knot requires

Table 2.2. The Social Attributes of Migrants

	Nonmigrants	Migrants	
	in 1970	in 1970	in 1980
% Middle Class	43	53	52
% Professional or White Collar[a]	37	52	50
% College	24	36	41
% High Income[b]	12	16	33
% Upwardly Mobile[c]	38	53	53

Source: American National Election Study, 1970; American National Election Study, 1980, Pre and Post Election Surveys, Center for Political Studies, University of Michigan.
[a]Head of household's occupation.
[b]Family income more than $30,000 in 1980; $10,000 in 1970.
[c]Upward social mobility based on occupation of head of household and respondent's father or family head.

twisting the data a bit and being clear about their implications. If those who migrated at an earlier time when measured later have significantly higher levels of socioeconomic standing or socioeconomic mobility, then migration may be more clearly associated with their improved situation.

The socioeconomic differences for migrants from the period 1964 to 1970 isolated in both the 1970 and 1980 data are shown in Table 2.2. Variables associated with socioeconomic status, subjective class, head of household's occupational status, and to a lesser degree education do not appear to shift over time within the 1970 migrant cohort. The evidence suggests that an individual's social status is set prior to migration; or put another way, migration does not seem to be associated with an increase in a migrant's socioeconomic standing.

A change in family income, however, has been shown in other research to be the main dividend for internal migration (Greenwood 1975:399–404). In a separate analysis, when the family income of 1970 migrants is compared to the income of nonmigrants of the period and controlled for age and head of household's occupational status, migrants appear to end up with higher family incomes by 1980.

Another way to test if migration influences broad socioeconomic attributes is to go back in time to a period prior to migration. One source of data used extensively in Chapter 6, the 1965–1973 Youth-Parent Panel Study (YP) data (see Appendix A for a description of these data), allows us to examine the nature of selected status attributes of eventual migrants.[2] Young adults were interviewed first in their last year of high school and reinterviewed at the age of twenty-five. From this set of respondents, those who migrated for any reason, including military service or to attend college, can be examined by before and after their migration. While many of the objective measures of occupations, income, and status are not appropriate evaluations for young high school seniors, they were asked extensive questions about their expected occupations some time in the future. Most of those who eventually migrated attained a level of class identification at the end of high school in 1965 which was comparable to the occupational categories they attained in 1973, the year of the second wave of the study. At twenty-five years of age, individuals are not old enough to determine their eventual occupational level, since those in their twenties have the highest rate of occupational mobility of any age group. In the five years prior to the 1970 Census, over 70 percent changed occupational categories, compared to 40 percent in their mid-thirties or forties. Nonetheless, lifelong, average socioeconomic status level is probably set by the mid-twenties. Education and not migration is considered the most important determinant of lifelong objective (Blau and Duncan 1967; Featherman and Hauser 1978) and subjective (Hodge and Treiman 1966) social status.

Whether educational attainment or eventual occupational or subjective social status are products of some form of anticipatory socialization is not clearly known. What an adolescent thinks his or her occupation will be may set up educational goals as well as a social class identification, even for an anticipated class. For instance, in the YP panel study, most of the social mobility that occurred from parents to children could be detected by the time the children were in their last year of high school. When the social status of a youth's occupational aspirations in 1965 is compared with the subjective social class, occupation, and education attained in 1973, the evidence suggests that those who appeared to be heading toward higher status occupations or advanced educations expected as much in 1965. Only 10 percent of the future middle class failed correctly to anticipate their future social class while still in high school. While there is considerable occupational mobility for those in their mid-twenties and after, their future seems to be bounded by earlier hopes and dreams or failures and resignations of adolescence.

Across measures of subjective personal economic outlook, for the present and the future, recent migrants are more optimistic than either nonmigrants or earlier migrants. As Table 2.3 illustrates, those who moved within the last five years are more likely to believe that they are doing better now than in the past and to expect to do better in the future. The expectations of those who migrated prior to 1974

Table 2.3. Subjective Retrospective and Prospective Assessment of Personal Financial Situation

	Migrated 1974–1980	Migrated before 1974	Nonmigrant	Total
Compared to a Year Ago				
% Better – % Worse	+7	−19	−8	−11
(N)	(361)	(612)	(342)	(1593)
Expected a Year from Now				
% Better – % Worse	+24	+3	+3	+8
(N)	(329)	(541)	(315)	(1437)
Income vs. Cost of Living				
% Rise – % Decline	−35	−45	−45	−41
(N)	(354)	(604)	(341)	(1568)

Source: American National Election Study, 1980, Pre and Post Election Surveys, Center for Political Studies, University of Michigan.

are in line with those of the nonmigrant population, in that they view their present and future economic well-being with more skepticism than is found among recent migrants.

Thus socioeconomic differences do exist among migrants in that those who moved more recently are likely to be drawn from relatively higher status groups and to be more optimistic about their financial condition. Over time their higher socioeconomic status recedes.

Political Attributes

Are there micropolitical differences between migrants, nonmigrants, and among different groups of migrants? If so, do the differences come about as a by-product of the migrants' relative youth, or as a result of their not having reached their full income potential based on their education and social status, factors of considerable importance for political participation? Or do the geographical aspects of migration, such as the distance of a move, rural to urban community changes, or interregional mobility, directly or indirectly influence the political attributes of migrants? Are the effects of the geographical attributes of a migration rooted in the age and socioeconomic differences among migrants from different places and regions? Or are the partisan and political commitment and participation differences a product of an elaborate, multistage process by which those who are left behind, or who have not yet moved, end up with different partisan values or different levels of commitment to politics and involvement in the electoral process?[3]

Migrants appear to reflect the contours of political commitment and the direction of partisan support one would expect from a random sample of the public. In 1980, 65 percent of the public were either strongly or weakly identified with one of the political parties. This was also true for 64 percent of those who had migrated. Across measures of psychological involvement in politics, turnout in elections, efforts to persuade others how to vote, and campaign involvement, migrants are not distinguishable from the total population. And when the consideration shifts to partisan support as measured by party identification and presidential or congressional vote, no significant differences emerge between the total population and migrants.

But when migrants are contrasted with nonmigrants, some interesting political differences seem to exist. On measures of commitment to politics, migrants tend to have a slightly lower level of strength of party attachment and participation in elections than nonmigrants. Yet no differences are found when migrants and nonmigrants are compared by the degree of psychological involvement in politics or by efforts to engage in political persuasion.

Measures of the directional support given to the parties or candidates of the major parties, however, do show differences between migrants and nonmigrants. Approximately 49 percent of the nonmigrants versus 40 percent of the migrants identified with the Democratic party in 1980. Nonmigrants voted at levels over 60 percent Democratic for congressional candidates, compared to just over 50 percent for migrants.

When those who migrated are separated by the recency of their migration, the differences found between all migrants and the nonmigrant population are accentuated. As Table 2.4 shows, the more recent migrants have a significantly weaker commitment to politics and a markedly lower propensity to become actively involved in the electoral process. This descriptive generalization is braced by the fact that recent migrants, when compared to nonmigrants, have a weaker attachment to parties, a lower turnout rate, and less interest in and concern with the outcome of elections. Recent migrants, however, do attempt to influence others politically at about the same level as do nonmigrants or the total population.

The differences between nonmigrants and the most recent migrants are in sharp contrast with the small differences between nonmigrants and those who had migrated at an earlier time, before 1974 in this case. Across the measures of political commitment, as

Table 2.4. Political Attributes of Migrant and Stable Populations

	Migrated 1974–1980	Migrated before 1974	Nonmigrant	Total
Commitment to Politics				
% Having Partisan Identification	59	68	68	65
(N)	(358)	(604)	(338)	(1550)
% High Psychological Involvement	19	24	21	21
(N)	(355)	(588)	(343)	(1534)
% Voting in 1980	54	66	65	62
(N)	(368)	(617)	(348)	(1586)
% Persuading Others How to Vote	33	34	33	29
(N)	(356)	(588)	(345)	(1537)
Direction of Partisan Support				
Party Identification PDI: % Dem – % Rep	+8	+23	+28	+18
(N)	(358)	(604)	(338)	(1550)
% Voted Same Party for President	46	43	45	42
(N)	(252)	(511)	(272)	(1240)
% Democratic Presidential Vote	47	54	56	52
(N)	(258)	(476)	(264)	(1178)
% Democratic Congressional Vote	47	54	65	54
(N)	(170)	(355)	(188)	(843)

Source: American National Election Study, 1980, Pre and Post Election Surveys, Center for Political Studies, University of Michigan.

Table 2.4 further shows, earlier migrants generally are linked in terms of their commitment to politics or to the political process at just about the same level as or even a slightly higher level than non-migrants.

From the evidence at hand, recent migrants are also different from nonmigrants and from early migrants across measures of partisan support. These migrants are somewhat less Democratic than non-migrants and earlier migrants based on party identification and con-gressional and presidential voting behavior. As before, earlier mi-grants appear to be very similar to nonmigrants by measures of the direction of their partisan support.

Are migrants in the late 1970s politically different from those who migrated before? In a similar vein to the cohort analysis done for

Table 2.5. Political Attributes of Migrants

	Nonmigrants	Migrants	
	in 1970	in 1970	in 1980
Commitment to Politics			
% Having Partisan Identification	71	61	65
% High Psychological Involvement	17	16	20
% Voting	59	41	66
% Persuading Others How to Vote	25	32	31
Direction of Partisan Support			
Party Identification PDI: % Dem – % Rep	+23	+11.3	+21
% Voted Same Party for President	60	57	46
% Dem Presidential Vote	nc[a]	nc	49
% Dem Congressional Vote	53	51	55

Source: American National Election Study, 1970; American National Election Study, 1980, Pre and Post Election Surveys, Center for Political Studies, University of Michigan.
[a]Insufficient cases.

socioeconomic change in the 1964 to 1970 migrants, the net change in that group's political attributes can be examined over a ten- to fifteen-year period. The evidence presented in Table 2.5 suggests that for the pre-1970 migrants, their degree of commitment to politics, while low compared to that of nonmigrants monitored in 1970, returned to the same levels as for those who had never migrated. In addition, their partisan orientations appear also to adjust toward the split found for the total population or for nonmigrants in 1980. As for their party identification, they became more Democratic than Republican. Their PDI (Percentage Difference Index) value in 1970 was +11 and increased to +21 by 1980. This represented a return to the Democratic level of nonmigrants in 1970, though it remained below the value (+28) found for nonmigrants in 1980. It is likely that the underlying political differences among migrants at the time of their migration and after are due to age-related and migration factors, and to their respective different socioeconomic attributes.

Mixed Roots of Migrant Politics

Internal migration is not usually a political act. It is not usually undertaken by people with political motives. Historical examples in which migrants crossed the country for purely political reasons are also rare. The concentration of Whigs, Republicans, or Democrats cannot account for even a small fraction of the stimulus for past geographical mobility.

It is possible that the social or economic conditions that stimulated some of the internal migration of the past may have been brought about by the policies pursued by local, state, or the federal government. Since the political history of the United States is riddled with officially sanctioned racial, religious, economic, and ethnic persecution, such practices and policies may have forced people from their homes and into new territories. The migration of the Mormons in the 1830s through Illinois and later to the Far West may be one of the foremost examples of migration as a result of religious persecution. Some of the migration of blacks from the South to the North must have resulted from the political and economic repression blacks experienced in the South both before and after Reconstruction. Yet even in this instance, politics and government policy played a role second to economic motives for migration (Lieberson 1980). (Black migration will be discussed further in the next chapter.) The most clear-cut example of when governmental policies induced migration was during the 1860s. Under the Morrill Land Grant and the Homestead Act, the federal government spurred western settlement by providing homestead sites at little or no monetary cost to the individual migrant. Occupancy for a certain period of time and a minimal fee were the only requirements for title.

In current times, the white flight from urban school districts to avoid forms of racial integration, however hard to document, shows that migration is still partially rooted in an individual's desire to avoid the ramifications of active or passive government policies.

Yet direct political concentration of population or specific government programs are not often the reasons that people migrate today. And by comparison to other countries where political factors have continually forced people to relocate or where refugees have become a constant source of political conflict, in the United States any direct political stimulus for internal migration is of secondary importance to nonpolitical factors. Net political effects of migration can only be determined when both migration related factors and socioeconomic factors are considered simultaneously.

What are these other geographical factors related to migration?

The distance of a migration, whether or not it involved a shift across a rural-urban demarcation, and whether a migrant entered or exited across regional boundaries and the South in particular—these are aspects of geographical mobility which can be linked to the socioeconomic and political attributes of the migrant (Hartman 1967).

One example is distance embodied in the classic statements of gravitational models of migration. Zipf's theory, for example, focused on the magnitude of the movement between two places. He argued that the total migration between two cities is directly related to their base population and inversely related to the distance between them (Zipf 1946:677–86). Stouffer suggested that interurban migration followed from the opportunities in the receiving areas and was inversely related to the possible intervening opportunities that migrants might encounter between receiving and supplying areas (Stouffer 1940:1–26).

The distance an individual moves, however, may be related to the social base of migration in terms of the intervening job opportunities available. Lansing and Mueller linked the distance of a migration directly to the individual's educational attainment and socioeconomic level (Lansing and Mueller 1967). They reasoned that those with less education face smaller labor markets, whereas those with higher education confront spatially larger markets in which to seek employment. A specialized background, like biophysics, means ferreting out one of a handful of jobs scattered throughout the nation (Ladinsky 1967:293–309; Leslie and Richardson 1961:874–902). This places a person in a labor market which extends across regions or even beyond national boundaries. A plumber, who does not have the same level of acquired technical knowledge, generally finds his craft in local demand. For a plumber, finding a market for his labor is often synonymous with deciding where to live. While the simple act of migration may not be highly correlated to the migrant's underlying socioeconomic traits, taking into account the distance of a migration may make the underlying socioeconomic differences among migrants more pronounced.

In addition, there is probably a threshold to the effect that distance of a move can have on an individual's migrating. A move from New York to Chicago, all things considered equally, is probably no different than one made from New York to Denver, even though Denver is further away from New York. Both are probably qualitatively different than moving from New York to Connecticut. Thus, stratifying by the distance of a migration may be a useful way of elaborating the social and political qualities of those migrating.

A case can be made for community size change and interregional mobility as important aspects of migration. Rural-to-urban migration, and its backflow, has been a central part of the migration experience in the United States. Often it has coincided with a change of geographical regions. Moving from a rural to an urban place and changing regions represent types of social contextual change in the way of life of a migrant and can have important political effects.

The Socioeconomic and Demographic Roots

Attempting to unravel the political correlates of internal migration given socioeconomic, demographic, and geographical factors stretches the limits of the sample survey data available if conducted with n-dimensional cross tabulations. There would simply not be enough respondents to perform the analysis. The problem is not new, and there are several clear alternatives to cross tabulations available that have proven effective for such analysis. The analysis which follows is summarized in Table 2.6 and uses multiple regression with dummy variables.[4]

The use of dummy variables is especially appropriate here because migration characteristics have qualitative distinctions. Shifts across county, state, and regional boundaries determine the effect of distance; movement within or across broadly defined lines of the urban and rural world is counted as a community size change. Regional migration means here movement within or across the South–non-South boundary. The dummy variables used capture these distinctions.

Measure of commitment to politics and direction of partisan support are the dependent variables. Each equation estimates the effect on the political attributes of an individual as a function of a set of socioeconomic and demographic variables: head of household occupation, occupational mobility, family income, subjective social class, age, and age minus age at time of migration.[5]

Table 2.6 summarizes the results of the multivariate equations. Each cell consists of a multiple correlation coefficient R^2 and an F statistic, to measure the significance of the migration factor. By reading across the table, the change in the contribution of migration experiences can be determined. For instance, in the first column the entries report the multiple correlation coefficients for a cross section of the total population. The second column gives the R^2 and the F statistic for the impact of migration status. The F statistic represents a ratio of how different are the R^2s between the cross section equation and the equation using migration status. If migration experience improves the explanation of migrants' political attributes, in part it would be reflected by an increase in the multiple correlation coefficient. If migration experience does not add significantly to the overall explained variance for the political attribute, the F statistic should be small.

From Table 2.6 the explanatory power of the different socioeconomic factors varies across the political dependent variables. Only 8 percent of the variation in the strength of party identification is explained by purely socioeconomic and age factors. Yet by the same estimation, 16 percent of the directional variance in party identification is explained.

The added predictive power of different migration experiences does not substantially add to the overall explained variation in individual political attributes. Beyond what is known from the socioeconomic or demographic characteristics of migrants, only eleven out of thirty-five of the equations that include an estimate of a migration effect have R^2s that differ significantly from the cross-sectional estimate.[6]

Regional migrations, especially those that cross the South–non-South boundary, are associated with a unique set of political attributes of migrants, even when socioeconomic and age factors are considered. The political cultures of the dominant geopolitical regions seem to prevail as important determinants of the strength of party attachment as well as of psychological and behavioral partisan support. Moreover, the joint effect of community size mobility and regional change is also a similar one. In addition, presidential vote in 1980 appears to be the only individual political attribute which induces an overall effect for any migration factor. (Why this can occur is discussed at the end of Chapter 5.) But what does seem clear is that the other migration factors—migration status, distance, and community size change—fail to have an impact on so many important facets of political behavior. Most aspects of human migration appear to lack any unique direct or indirect relevance to the political attributes of those who experience them. It appears that migration has only weak effects on the politics of individuals. Does this mean that the migration phenomenon, per se, has little political significance?

Certain migration experiences are clearly linked to an individual's politics. Regional migration when accompanied by rural-to-urban change shows clear ties to an individual migrant's political attributes. Of course, regional migration and subsequent shifts from rural to urban areas represent dramatic instances when political boundaries may be crossed. Traditionally such movement has been assumed to

Table 2.6. Summary of Differences between Cross-Sectional and Migrant Samples by Political Attributes Regressed by Social Background[a]

	Migration Experience					
	R^2 Total Population	R^2 Migrant Status	R^2 Distance Mobility	R^2 Size Mobility	R^2 Region Mobility	R^2 Region & Size Mobility
Commitment to Politics						
Strength of Party Identification	.08062	.08342 (2.49)[b]	.08153 (0.41)	.08681 (1.87)	.08927 (2.57)*	.09663 (2.89)*
Psychological Involvement	.07942	.08388 (3.97)*	.07964 (0.10)	.08141 (0.58)	.08478 (1.57)	.08657 (1.27)
Turnout in 1980	.14076	.14201 (1.19)	.14288 (0.67)	.14305 (0.72)	.14103 (0.08)	.14349 (0.52)
Direction of Partisan Support						
Party Identification	.15614	.15669 (0.53)	.15881 (1.29)	.15758 (0.46)	.17002 (4.54)*	.17224 (4.00)*
Voted for Same Party in Past	.07371	.07357 NA	.07390 (0.09)	.07468 (0.28)	.07543 (0.50)	.07693 (0.56)
Presidential Vote	.14270	.16154 (15.12)*	.16237 (7.83)*	.16288 (5.38)*	.17042 (7.45)*	.17374 (6.12)*
Congressional Vote	.11110	.11110 (0)	.11600 (1.63)	.11288 (0.40)	.13051 (4.37)*	.13319 (2.70)

Source: American National Election Study, 1980, Pre and Post Election Surveys, Center for Political Studies, University of Michigan.

[a]The constant independent variables entered in the regression equation are: race, head of household, occupation, occupational mobility, family income, subjective class, religion, age, and age minus age moved. Occupational mobility, religion and age were constructed as dummy variables to allow a linear estimation. Equations were calculated based on an OLS model.

[b] $$F = \frac{[R^2 \text{ (with migration experience)} - R^2 \text{ (Cross section)}] / k - 1}{[1 - R^2 \text{ (with migration experience)}] / N - k - 1}$$

where

k = number of dummy variables used to determine *migration* effect

R^2 = the multiple correlation coefficient from equation summarized in Table 2.5

*p is less than .05

place migrants in situations where they experience clear political change because of the different political cultures associated with certain rural areas, especially those in the South.

In the next chapter we will examine the major historical population movement streams that have dominated the nature of geographical mobility and have often been associated with changes in political environments.

Summary

With cross-sectional surveys from the 1970 and 1980 National Election Studies (NES), comparisons were made of all migrants, nonmigrants, and recent versus past migrants.

1. The main socioeconomic and political differences are found between migrants and nonmigrants. Those differences increase when recent migrants are considered and diminish in intensity for earlier migrants. The socioeconomic differences suggest that migrants, especially at the time of migration, are more likely to come from a slightly higher socioeconomic segment than do nonmigrants.
2. Over time, however, family income seems to be the sole dividend of migration.
3. Recent migrants are less committed to political parties and less likely to vote than nonmigrants. When recent migrants participate, they are also more pro-Republican than nonmigrants, earlier migrants, or the total population. Over time, they appear to look more like the total population and nonmigrants.
4. A multivariate analysis shows that unless an identifiable political change is also associated with the migration, such as a move across a regional boundary, socioeconomic and age characteristics of migrants account for most of the observed effects of internal migration on migrants' political actions and values.

Let us now turn to a closer examination of some of the effects of migration which do appear to be obviously associated with the political attributes of migrants.

Chapter 3

Migration Streams

> The claim pinches out, the grass dies, the well dries
> up, and everyone will ride off to form up again
> somewhere else for me to travel. Nothing fixes in
> this damn country, people blow around at the whiff
> of the wind. You can't bring the law to a bunch of
> rocks, you can't settle the coyotes, you can't make a
> society out of sand. I sometimes think we're worse
> than the Indians. . . . What is the name of this
> place?
>
> —E. L. Doctorow, *Welcome to Hard Times*

Migration in America was once very exciting. The Reverend Doctor Doddridge, in his description of frontier life, said that the first to arrive were woodsmen. Most were trying to get away from creditors. They survived by living like Indians. Every few years they would move further out as civilization—other settlers—encroached. Dirt farmers came next. They lived like woodsmen but tended their farms better. Farmers came next. Most were Protestants who came to stay, to build towns and to raise children. They brought commerce, civil order, and stability to the American frontier (Doddridge 1783). On the frontier, boom areas attracted many times the population that eventually settled there. In all likelihood, the origin of permanent, two-way flows of population started with the movements of early settlers in and out of the frontier.

While the composition of the migrants can change as an area de-velops, these aggregate geographical streams are surprisingly constant. Migration to the Far West, the North-South population exchange, and the circulation of the population through the urban world are important, well-known aspects of American migration. Each is described in this chapter in terms of the socioeconomic, partisan, and in some instances participatory attributes of those moving, those staying behind, and those in the place of destination. We ask, How regular is the composition of the aggregate stream? What political change do migrants within these population movement streams experience over time?

Migration West

As the population of the United States grew from 5 million at the turn of the eighteenth century, it migrated West. Although the definition of the West today is very specific, as recently as a hundred years ago, the West was a fluid, elastic concept without a clear demarcation line. In 1800, the population of the United States was distributed evenly between the Northeast and the South. Then, as today, certain regions and places were capable either of supplying population or of receiving it. In the 1800s, New England and the eastern states were threatened by westward migration. Opposition from the original colonies to the Louisiana Purchase rested on the fear that they would be emptied by out-migration. As it turned out, their reasoning was sound; between 1810 and 1816, Ohio grew in population from 230,000 to 400,000.

Following the opening of the Northwest Territory, the westward expansion accelerated. By 1850, the territory of the midwestern states contained nearly one quarter of the total population of the United States, and by 1870, it was equal to the Northeast and the South in absolute population size (Taeuber and Taeuber 1958:5–6.).

The following fifty years brought the expansion of the population across the Mississippi and closer to today's Far West. In 1880, approximately 3.5 million persons moved west across the Mississippi. This period, however, turned out to be the West's high-water mark in the population increase due to net migration, the difference between in-migration and out-migration. From 1900 on, the number of those moving west of all those born east of the midcontinent gradually declined. The growth of the West as a consequence has relied less on in-migration and more on natural population increase: births over deaths and the influx of new waves of immigrants. And in spite of a post–World War II boom in California and the later increases in some

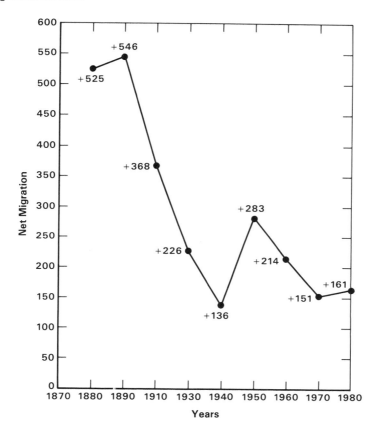

Figure 3.1

Migration to the West[a]

Source: Irene Taeuber, 1972, "The Changing Distribution of the
Population of the United States in the Twentieth Century," in volume 5
of *Population Distribution and Policy*, ed. Sara Mills Mazie (Washington,
D.C.: U.S. Commission on Population Growth and the American Future).

[a]Net migration is in-migration minus out-migration per 1,000 population,
aged 25 to 44 at the end of each decade from 1870 to 1980.

southwestern states, the rate of net migration to the Far West has
declined steadily from the turn of the century.[1] (See Figure 3.1.)

The steady erosion of the rate of net migration to the Far West
follows the degree to which the Far West's economic picture became
tied to that of the rest of the nation. Even California, once the bright
spot of economic growth, exhibited by the late 1970s a growth in real
income that was no different from that of the rest of the nation. Has

the decline in population growth due to migration and the alteration and slowdown in economic growth changed the composition of the in-migration streams? We will now take a look at the composition of the movement streams to the West.

Sociopolitical Attributes of Westward Migrants

In the post–World War II period, over half of all those migrating to a new region migrated to the Far West. By 1970, 25 percent of the West was composed of native westerners; 44 percent were from the Midwest or the Northeast, and 30 percent were from the South.

From the very beginning, those living in the West from the North and South were politically different from each other, from those they left behind, and from those originally from the West. Early research stressed that both sets of migrants to the West, in spite of the suspension of the social and political supports of their nurturing political cultures, retained their original political persuasions. Few recalled changing their party allegiance. And presidential vote comparisons between the Far West migrants and those remaining in the supplying regions failed to show any diminution of original party attachment. Northern migrants were predominately Republican. The southerners who moved West remained politically aligned with the Democrats as did those who stayed in the South (Campbell et al. 1960:chap. 16).

The social composition of in-migrants to the West has changed. When the new waves of immigrants from Mexico, Central America, and Asia are ignored, the social status of new arrivals has risen over time. In total, those arriving in the western states after 1960 are more middle class, better educated, richer, and employed in higher professional or managerial occupations than migrants in previous decades. Based on objective status measures, this cross-temporal difference stems from a widening of the socioeconomic differences between the southern and the northern in-migrants and not from a secular rise in the composition of migrants from each stream. When the post-1960 migration streams are partitioned by region of origin, the shift upward in the social status of migrants to the West is seen as the product of different northern migrants arriving in the West.

Figure 3.2 shows the social status composition of migrants from the South and North who moved to the Far West. These population movement streams have been divided into periods before 1960, between 1962 and 1970, after 1970. The majority of migrants moved to the West after 1945 at the close of World War II.[2] Prior to 1960, northern migrants to the West as a group are higher in objective social status than are southern migrants. And while the composition of the

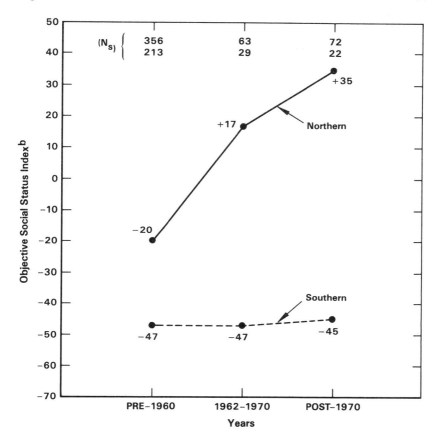

Figure 3.2

The Social Base of Migration to the West[a]

Source: American National Election Studies, 1952–1980, Center for Political Studies, University of Michigan.

[a]Pre-1960 PDI scores are based on pooled NES studies (1952-1960). 1962–1970 PDI scores are based on pooled NES studies (1962–1970). Post-1972 PDI scores are based on pooled NES studies (1972–1980).

[b]See Appendix A.2 for definition of the Objective Social Status Index.

migration stream from the South has remained constant, the stream of migrants from the North has been composed increasingly of citizens with a higher social status. The gap between these two migration streams in terms of their social and economic composition has increased over time.

Before 1960 and after, southerners moving to the West were

largely drawn from blue collar and service occupations or from groups whose education ended well before college. Even when the southern blacks moving to the urban centers of the West are excluded, the whites from the South populated the bottom of an objective status ladder.[3]

The American Voter (Campbell et al. 1960) argues that the political differences in the pre-1960 groups resulted not only from differing patterns of early political socialization but also from the socioeconomic attributes which distinguish southerners and northerners. A third of the northern in-migrants were employed in professional or white collar occupations, as compared to only a quarter of the southern in-migrants. Those from the South had lower educational levels and consequently were locked into a lower income scale, even in relatively prosperous areas. Such increasingly greater socioeconomic differences between southern and northern migrants could lead to even sharper political differences. But before turning to a discussion of the compositional change in westward migrants, let us take a closer look at the political traits of migrants to the West in the period prior to 1960.

The political attributes of several relevant western groups are shown in Table 3.1. The migrant groups are broken down by their region of origin and by when they migrated. For comparative purposes, the composition of the native populations in the West, South, and North are also illustrated.[4]

The regional political milieu within which migrants move is an important consideration to the potential effect of diverse population streams on an area's political culture. In the period prior to 1960, the western region was politically between the South and the North. When westerners are compared to those native to the other regions prior to 1960, their partisan attributes appear midway between the one-party Democratic dominated South and the more balanced, but still pro-Republican, North, as Table 3.1 shows.

There are several historical reasons for this situation. One is the West's nonpartisan heritage. A single political party never had the power it enjoyed in some eastern urban areas or southern rural counties. And western states were quick to adopt the electoral laws and institutions of the populist era. At once these reforms provided a series of mechanisms for nonpartisan elections, and later for the attenuation of the organizational development and growth of the political parties.[5]

The West's migrant populations from both the South and the North, however, match the broad partisan categories of their originating regions. In the pre-1960 period, the southerners in the West were Democratic, though not as Democratic as those they had left

Table 3.1. Political Attributes of Migration Streams to the Far West

	Grew Up in the South migrated		Grew Up in the North migrated		Native West		Native South		Native North	
	pre-1960[a]	post-1960[b]	pre-1960	post-1960	pre-1960	post-1960	pre-1960	post-1960	pre-1960	post-1960
Party Identification										
PDI: % Dem – % Rep	+22	+39	+19	+9	+30	+13	+55	+38	−1	+6
(N)	(155)	(64)	(366)	(179)	(650)	(1727)	(2525)	(4559)	(5384)	(8814)
Congressional Vote										
% Dem	55	80	48	51	62	52	80	71	44	79
(N)	(89)	(25)	(213)	(88)	(415)	(1030)	(1182)	(1951)	(3948)	(5123)
Presidential Vote										
% Dem	47	57	43	33	47	44	52	40	38	47
(N)	(71)	(21)	(188)	(63)	(385)	(702)	(1162)	(1402)	(3374)	(3548)

Source: American National Election Studies, 1952–1980, Center for Political Studies, University of Michigan.

[a] Pre-1960 scores are based on pooled NES data from 1952 to 1960.

[b] Post-1960 scores are based on pooled NES data from 1964 to 1980 for migrants entering their current state after 1960.

behind. Southerners living in the West were also less Democratic than the native westerners on two out of three measures of party support and equally Democratic on the third measure. With regional-level measures of political environment, of course, it is impossible to speculate if the migrants from the South were adapting to a less Democratic political environment than they left, were drawn from places with a more competitive party system than is generally attributed to the South during that period, or were composed of less partisan migrants.

The north-to-west stream was more Republican than its Southern counterpart, though not by much. If 5 percent is considered a significant percentage difference, then only in terms of their congressional voting were the northerners more Republican than the southerners in the West (Goodman, 1964). Moreover, those who had migrated from the eastern and midwestern states were significantly *less* Republican than those who did not.

The pre-1960 pattern of the westward migrant's partisan loyalties is not simply a product of the social base of the different migration streams. Native southerners were significantly higher in status (PDI = +3) than south-to-west migrants. Native northerners were lower in social status (PDI = −26) than were migrants from the North moving to the West.

During the post-1960 period, the partisan differences between the migration streams to the West intensified. Table 3.1 further illustrates that southerners entering the West after 1960 were still more Democratic than those from the North. They were also significantly more Democratic than native westerners and northerners. The declining support of the native southern white population for the Democratic party, especially in the elections after 1964, seems not to be influenced by the partisan tendencies of those migrating to the West.

The northern stream also changed. In the twenty years over which the partisan support estimates measure, the partisan identification and presidential support of the northern migration stream became clearly more Republican. Somewhat out of step with this pro-Republican swing, the congressional vote of the post-1960 north-to-west stream remained virtually unchanged.

The broad regional contexts within which this stream moved also shifted. Native northerners became more Democratic over time while the native West became more Republican. But again, the partisan inclinations of the northern migration stream do not match either the host or the supplying region. The observed change in northern and southern migration streams to the Far West has accentuated their partisan differences, and as will be seen, may have important long-term consequences for the West's politics.

What happens to those who end up living in the West? Are their patterns of social mobility the same? Do they maintain their political distinctions? As we have already shown above, those who migrate to the West are not strictly politically representative of their originating region, nor are they politically similar to those native to the West. The consequences of interregional migration for their partisanship take shape when comparisons are made of the pre-1960 migrants both before 1960 and in the years after. If migrants do not change over time, cross-sectional pre-1960 cohorts should have partisan attributes identical to those of migrants who moved West before 1960 but who were interviewed in the years after 1964.

Though any cohort evidence is circumstantial, a picture of migrants changing politically by adjusting their behavior and attitudes emerges from the comparisons made between the 1950s and the late 1970s. As Table 3.2 shows, migrants who entered the West before 1960 but who were interviewed in the years after 1964 show some differences across socioeconomic and political measures as compared with the same group when interviewed in the 1950s.

Within the specific tracking streams, southerners show only a modest increase in their social standing after living in the West a number of years. Most ex-southerners remained lower in social status absolutely and relative to northern migrants. Living in the West did not reverse ex-southerners' pro-Democratic inclinations. Over time, the Democratic identification of south-to-west migrants increased. The initial partisan support of southern migrants to the West for the Democratic party's congressional and presidential candidates also increased.

Southern migrants' partisan orientations may be tied to political values set by early socialization. But their political development does not appear similar to that of southern nonmigrants. From previous research, one expectation would be that whites who had migrated from the South would continue to respond to national political forces in a fashion similar to that of other southerners (Campbell et al. 1960:chap. 16; Converse et al. 1969). This does not appear to be the case.

White southerners who remained in the South have moved away from the Democratic party. In Table 3.1 the net shift across the three measures of party support shows the native South moving to a less Democratic stance. In the pre-1960 to post-1960 period, southerners declined by over 10 percent in their support for congressional candi-

Table 3.2. Change in the Sociopolitical Attributes of the Pre-1960 Western Migrant Cohort

	Grew Up in the South			Grew Up in the North		
	t_1[a]	t_2[b]	$\Delta\ t_2 - t_1$	t_1	t_2	$\Delta\ t_2 - t_1$
Objective Social Status						
PDI: % High – % Low	− 36	− 24	+ 12	− 15	+ 21	+ 36
(N)	(168)	(152)		(367)	(367)	
Party Identification						
PDI: % Dem – % Rep	+ 22	+ 48	+ 21	+ 19	+ 11	− 7
(N)	(155)	(151)		(366)	(361)	
Congressional Vote						
% Dem	55	68	+ 13	48	55	+ 7
(N)	(89)	(75)		(213)	(251)	
Presidential Vote						
% Dem	47	61		43	41	− 2
(N)	(71)	(70)		(188)	(175)	

Source: American National Election Studies, 1952–1980, Center for Political Studies, University of Michigan.

[a] Pre-1960 scores are based on pooled NES data from 1952 to 1960 for white respondents migrating to the West prior to 1960.

[b] Post-1960 scores are based on pooled NES data from 1964 to 1980 for respondents migrating to the West prior to 1960.

dates and 12 percent in their support for Democratic presidential candidates; their identification with the Democratic party relative to their identification with the Republican party also declined. Southerners living in the Far West have shifted in the other direction to a stronger commitment to the Democrats. Why? One explanation might be the difference in the racial climates of the West and the South. Southerners migrating before 1960 were not exposed directly to the civil rights movement that began in earnest after 1960. Southerners in the West did not directly experience the racial tensions and political conflict that followed. These regional political forces clearly contributed to the shift of whites out of the southern Democratic party. Of course, we do not know for the migrants involved in this analysis the differences in their local political environments or the degree of change of local environments they experienced by migrating.

Those migrating from the North offer a different pattern of response. Northerners prospered in the West. As indicated by the Objective Social Status Index, they moved from an average PDI score of − 15 before 1960 to + 21 thereafter. A class-based expectation would be that their upward social mobility would induce in them a more pro-Republican stance in national politics. The cohort moving before 1960 did not, however, increasingly embrace the Republican party. Northerners in the West remained more Democratic than Republican. Their partisanship development, however, appears to have been attenuated by migration. This seems apparent especially when they are compared to southern migrants, who increasingly grew more Democratic, to those nonmigrants remaining in the North, who also became more pro-Democratic; and to the native western population, which in terms of party identification and congressional vote, became less Democratic.

Rural-to-Urban Migration

From the earliest periods, the pushing forces of economic adversity and the pulling forces of prosperity seem to have generated the net flow of populations. In the United States, during the initial settlement period, the population dispersed West into *rural* areas, open country and farms, as a function of vast agricultural opportunities. The first phase was nearly completed by the mid-1880s, although rural areas continued to increase in number until the end of the nineteenth century.

Internal migration has also coincided with the population growth in urban areas. Historically American cities are thought to have grown primarily as the result of foreign immigration. While foreign immigrants contributed to urban growth, however, foreign immigration is not a sufficient causal factor. The urbanization of society also resulted from the change from an agricultural to an industrial economic base, and consequently from a rural to a metropolitan orientation (see Taeuber and Taeuber 1958:106–9; Shryock 1964:295–301).

Technology and transportation were part of the reason rural dwellers moved to urban areas. Production equipment changed from hand-held tools used by artisans in towns and villages to machines in large factories, which could take advantage of an economy of scale. Early industrial manufacturing relied on coal and iron ore as fuel and resources, which limited the location of factories. Railroads were the primary means for transporting material resources to industries and finished goods to markets. Railway lines created new forms of industry and opened up new markets and centers of commerce. In places where railroads converged, industry and population grew (Easterlin 1980:chap. 4).

Economic trends were also associated with urbanization. The income available to the average consumer increased in metropolitan areas. Consumers and workers with more disposable income per capita spent it on nonagricultural products, thus encouraging commercial activity. Consumer demand increased industrial activity and the applications of technology to business. Service sector industries evolved, which in turn created more jobs. Job opportunities expanded and demand for labor grew. Each aspect of industrial growth fed the other. The by-product of all this was the concentration of population.

The pull of opportunities for employment in an expanding urban industrial area was aided by the depopulation of rural communities caused by a change in farm technology. Mechanization and subsequent expansion of farming productivity required fewer farmers. After 1900, ten sons went to the city for every one who was able to start a farm (Shannon 1945:31–37; Hauser and Duncan 1959). The children of farmers were simply pushed out.

Natural increases in urban areas and the reclassification of towns to cities were less important to early urbanization. The birth rates in cities lagged far behind the rural areas. In the United States, even as late as 1930, urban women had 41 percent fewer children than did rural women. Developing areas, when compared to rural America especially during the turn of the twentieth century, also had significantly higher mortality rates. Rural-to-urban migration was the real source of growth of the urban sector (Hauser and Duncan 1959).

Detailed internal migration data are not reliable prior to 1920. Yet much of the urban growth that did occur was attributed to migrants coming from the farm. This observation is supported by the aggregate population shift. The proportion of farmers, the most visible element of the rural society, declined from 30 percent of the population in 1930 to 6 percent in 1970. When this trend is coupled with the growth of cities, the presumption is that farmers and their children populated the cities. But the 1950 census maps a different path. Of the 1.8 million who were estimated to have left farms during the preceding year, less than half went to cities. Over 42 percent went to other residences in the open country or to unincorporated hamlets. Of the 43 percent who went to cities, only a fraction went to urbanized areas. Farmers, it seems, followed a curious path of least resistance and disruption. Migrants from the rural world leave in steps and over several generations. And as will be seen below, when they finally get to urban areas they or their descendants appear gradually to turn around and go back.

As late as 1970, 60 percent of all migrants described the areas they grew up in as rural. But in the 1980s, around 70 percent of the population live in urban areas or in their surrounding suburbs. Thus the temporal proximity of rural experiences plus the dominance today of the urban life make rural-to-urban migration an important aspect of American life. Of course, whether this type of migration has political meaning is the question at hand.

The Composition of Northern Migrants to the Cities

Rural-to-urban migration has been represented as an example of push-pull induced migration (Kutznetz 1957). Individuals will migrate to prosperous areas when the economic conditions decline in the area in which they currently live. In rural areas migration has occurred supposedly because of the gradual decline in the demand for agricultural labor, the push, and the rise in the demand for industrial labor, the pull. The implications of a push-pull model are clear. How far these individuals migrate and the consequences of their migration are variables which have been vigorously analyzed (Zipf 1946; Stouffer 1940; Carrothers 1956; Isard 1960:chap. 11; Olson 1965). Rural migrants are therefore assumed to be from the bottom of the social structure, less educated with low incomes. They are assumed to be bound for low-status occupations.

Northern ruralites entered urban areas mainly during and immediately after the Second World War. Their migration contributed to the last phase of urban growth in the North. Like some former ruralites, northerners who migrated to the cities before 1960 were from the lower segments of the social strata, as Table 3.3 shows.[6]

Compared to lifelong rural dwellers, migrants from rural places are drawn from considerably higher status backgrounds and attained higher levels of socioeconomic stature. When the confounding factors of region and race are stripped away, northern rural-to-urban migrants dispel some of the expectations of a push-pull model. Before 1960, migrants were a representative cross section of the rural population. After 1960, they were from the upper end.

Other historical analysis also fails to uphold the push-pull model. Eldridge shows that those reaching the ages of twenty to twenty-four at the end of prosperous decades between 1870 and 1950 have rates of migration which peak earlier than those aged twenty to twenty-four at the end of depressed decades. That is, net migration tends to slow down rather than speed up during periods of economic decline (Eldridge 1964). During the 1930s when farm areas were more severely affected by the Depression, the rate of rural out-migration actually lowered.

Lansing and Mueller examined the movement out of depressed areas and compared it with the geographical mobility from places which did not have higher and persistent unemployment or a high percentage of low income families. What they report is that actual out-migration or expectations about future migration are unrelated to an area's economic situation. If anything, those in areas which are marginally worse off economically have a slightly lower rate of out-migration (Lansing and Mueller 1967).

Economic hardship precludes the resources an individual needs to pick up and move. Those from rural areas who moved to more urban places in all likelihood had a surplus of human capital. Thus the hand of economic adversity only weakly pushes individuals to migrate.

While the evidence for the pushing forces of economic decline seems thin, there is rather strong evidence that pulling factors of economic growth are important causes of migration (Greenwood 1975). Migration is most likely to occur between places which are vibrant centers of economic growth (Lansing and Mueller 1967). The exact reason for this asymmetry is not clear. One reason might be that in a very short period of time, the mobile leave depressed areas, and since few enter, there is no one else to leave. Another reason could be that places that experience economic decline serious enough to induce migration fail to provide the competitive educational opportunities and occupational skills needed by residents to take advantage of opportunities elsewhere (Todaro 1969; Lansing and Morgan 1967). And finally the out-of-pocket moving costs for someone unemployed and in a declining area may simply preclude migration as a viable alternative to staying and marginally making ends meet (Lansing and Mueller 1967). Thus the notion that migrants are unemployed or between jobs or solely from impoverished areas is not an accurate one.

While there is not strong evidence for a push-pull model of aggregate population movement, economic factors remain important causes of migration, especially that from rural to urban areas. More than 60 percent of the heads of families who moved over a five-year period gave economic considerations as the main reason for migration (Sell 1983:305). Of those moving for economic reasons, nearly 40 percent do so for higher pay and a better chance of occupational advancement, 25 percent because they were transferred to another job, and only 20 percent to find a job, enter the labor force, or get full-time work (Lansing and Mueller 1967).

In spite of their relatively low socioeconomic standing compared to others in urban areas, former ruralites have pro-Republican partisan orientations. As Table 3.3 shows, the composition of rural-urban migrants was solidly Republican both before and after 1960. Their political loyalties matched those traditionally associated with the rural northeast and north central areas of the country during the period. The stable rural population during the period in question remained Republican and appeared nearly identical politically to those who migrated to the cities.

In the years after 1960, urban in-migrants were significantly higher in socioeconomic standing than either the previous migration stream or those who stayed in the rural areas. By 1970, half of the rural-urban migrants suggested that they were middle class when asked for a class identification. Over 50 percent were employed in professional or white collar occupations, and nearly a third had finished a college education. The rural population during the period after 1960, on the other hand, has shown little change in terms of objective social status and education measures, but the socioeconomic status of the rural-to-urban migration stream has continued to increase into the 1980s.

The political composition of urban in-migrants remained virtually unchanged over time. After 1960, as Table 3.3 shows, the rural-urban migrants remained linked to the Republican party. Analysis at separate time points shows that their pro-Republican traits increased. In 1970, approximately 40 percent identified with the Democratic party. By 1980, this proportion had dropped to 28 percent. The proportion voting for Democratic congressional candidates also declined between 1970 and 1980 from 46 percent to 40 percent.

Earlier studies suggested that rural northern migrants were impervious to their changed political environments. Shifts in the size and type of community were given clear political interpretations, at least when monitored in the 1950s. Changes from rural communities assumed to be politically Republican to urban places assumed to be Democratic did not induce migrants to alter their partisan support or behavior. Republican ruralites who moved to the cities remained Republican assembly-line workers and passed their identifications on to their children. And when they acquired the means to do so, they exited metropolitan places for suburbs or nonmetropolitan areas (Campbell et al. 1960).

Resistance of ruralites to the pressures of urban settings (with their presumed political cultures) has not been reported in other countries. Miller and Stouthard (1974) found that confessional attachment in the Netherlands is "heavily influenced by established local group norms of behavior and will change as residential movement confronts a person with a new set of norms." Valen and Katz (1964:169) show in Norway that rural-to-urban movement results from a desired upward mobility for farmers and other rural persons

Table 3.3. The Sociopolitical Attributes of Urban and Rural White Populations in the North

	Rural to Urban		Stable Urban		Stable Rural		Pre-1960 Migrants
							$\Delta t_2 - t_1$[c] Rural to Urban
	Pre-1960[a]	Post-1960[b]	Pre-1960	Post-1960	Pre-1960	Post-1960	
Objective Social Status							
PDI: % High − % Low	−31 (1723)	+15 (1294)	−20 (2375)	+32 (1337)	−34 (1110)	−35 (485)	+12
Party Commitment							
Party Identification							
PDI: % Dem − % Rep	−1 (1689)	0 (1284)	+10 (2352)	+9 (1358)	−2 (1072)	−1 (458)	+7
Congressional Vote							
% Dem	46% (1164)	49% (653)	50% (1695)	49% (706)	45% (747)	39% (195)	+6
Presidential Vote							
% Dem	37% (972)	37% (486)	43% (1457)	42% (566)	35% (565)	36% (174)	+3

Source: American National Election Studies, 1952–1980, Center for Political Studies, University of Michigan.
[a] Same as Table 3.1.
[b] Same as Table 3.1.
[c] Same as Table 3.2.

seeking a better life in the cities. The rural-to-urban migration in Norway produced dramatic alterations in partisan attachment and voting behavior. In Sweden the growth of the Social Democratic Party from the early 1900s on coincided with the growth of cities and towns. It has been suggested that the increased support of this party was partially due to the effective attraction of rural migrants who previously had no visible ties to a party (Lewin et al. 1972; Särlvik 1974).

Why have rural-to-urban migrants from the North failed to change? Part of the reason usually given is that class factors important to politics and industrialization have not been as central to electoral decisions in the United States as in Europe (Hartz 1955). Yet part of the reason may lie in the contextual change experienced by rural-to-urban migrants. If the immediate environments into which they migrated were the same as those they left, they would not be expected to change partisan values.

From the evidence at hand, northern rural in-migrants appear to have been influenced by the predominately pro-Democratic urban climate of opinion. Again in Table 3.3, the difference measures for the pre-1960 migrants show a clear pattern of increasing pro-Democratic behavior and attitudes. This trend occurs even though, as a group, former ruralites have experienced a significant increase in their objective socioeconomic standing.

Unlike blacks and whites from the rural South, northern urban in-migrants participate politically at rates normally expected for their socioeconomic status grouping. Across measures of turnout and participation in campaigns, they are involved in the electoral process at rates more or less comparable to those whites who have always lived in cities, and similar to those left in the rural communities (Verba and Nie 1972:237–42).

Urban-to-Rural Migration

Net migration is the product of several movement streams. Some migrants move in precisely the opposite direction of the majority. And in time some counter-streams become the new dominant direction of population movement. Counter-movements of population may also portend important social and political changes.

In the United States rural back flow was first the product of the fluctuations in the demand for labor in industry. When recessions or depressions occurred, many ex-ruralites returned to their original communities and family homes. There they could live cheaply and wait to return to their jobs. The depression in the 1930s illustrates this point. The rate of rural out-migration not only slowed, but people actually returned to farms, as well as small towns and rural villages. In 1920, 30 percent of the population was in farming. This level continued to drop in 1930 to 24.9 percent, but increased to 25.8 percent in 1933. The small percentage change in the population reflected 1,844,000 people moving back to farms over a brief three-year period (Taeuber and Taeuber 1958).

World War II also played an important role in spurring on nonmetropolitan residential preferences. For nearly half a decade, hundreds of thousands of Americans were confined to a very regimented life. Following the war, the opportunity to acquire a single-family dwelling was greatly enhanced by the guaranteed home loan program under the GI Bill of Rights. The forms of residential living that may have developed if the war had not occurred are not known. But it seems clear that to own a home was the culmination of dreams formed under efficient but harsh conditions.

The widespread ownership of the automobile was also an important factor in nonurban growth. Those industries able to produce automobiles for individualized transportation from home to job also expanded as a result of the war effort. The greatly increased post-war capacity of the automobile industry to produce a car or two per family freed the individual from the ties of mass public transportation often necessary in the urban setting. All of this, when coupled with the obvious tax advantage given to homeowners, contributed to the growth of the nonurban setting.

It was not until the mid-1960s that urban-to-rural migration became a major, permanent counter-stream in the United States. In the 1970s the rural, nonmetropolitan areas gained continuously in population. From 1970 to 1978, rural areas in the United States received over 3 million more people than they lost. In 1980, the net migration continued to nonmetropolitan areas. And with the decline in fertility in the rural sector, the rate of in-migration became an important component of rural community growth (U.S. Bureau of the Census 1983; Taeuber 1972).

Of migrants to rural areas, most traditionally have been returnees (Zuiches 1981). Yet after 1970, a new migration stream began to enter nonmetropolitan areas. Half to 60 percent were traditional urbanites, migrants whose families were from urban rather than farming backgrounds. They represent migrants whose residential preference is for rural areas. Since 1948, half of a national sample of those asked have stated that they prefer to live in small towns or very rural areas (Mazie 1972).

The reason people prefer living in nonmetropolitan areas are not difficult to understand. Many urbanites have strong emotional ties to the rural world. Beliefs and memories of the quality of life associated with the farm or small town are part of modern folklore.

Unlike many caricatures, the atavistic view of rural living may even contain some reality. Whether one considers the quality of local schools and the low rate of crime or the ambience of an area as a place to live, rural places are often perceived as providing a better quality of life (Campbell et al. 1976:236). The coupling of wishful myths with some reality makes the rural setting a powerful pulling force.

What Emptied Cities?

Once the central city was a place where jobs existed for those whose only resource was their labor. Work in early industries was dirty, dangerous, and poorly paid. Jobs were for the unskilled, the illiterate, the immigrant. Required skills could be learned quickly. And if an employer or foreman was not satisfied with the worker, there was always someone else to hire. Because of jobs, American cities were like magnets to rural or foreign populations.

Entry-level jobs today, however, are often the product of public policy. CETA and other past job programs have replaced the garment, steel, manufacturing, and automobile industries as places where the basic job skills are learned (Chamberlain, Cullen, and Lewin 1980).

The urban core has not retained the employment opportunities needed to support a diverse population. While some central cities are experiencing a growth in commercial centers, in most there has been a flight of capital investment. City centers are of diminished importance as centers for the financial or even the service sector, both of which tend to follow population concentrations (Sternlieb and Hughes 1980). And finally the development of new technology in industry is largely taking place outside of metropolitan areas. Central cities have been left by those able to leave, much like rural areas were a hundred years ago.

Sociopolitical Attributes of the Exiting Urbanites

While rural-to-urban migrants show political adaptation, it might be simply a by-product of selective out-migration from cities by earlier rural-to-urban migrants or their children. A Republican circulation through the cities has been pointed to in the past (Campbell et al. 1960). Higher status Republicans were leaving the cities in the 1950s. And the urban Republican holdovers were those locked in at the bottom of the socioeconomic hierarchy. That they may have shifted their identification toward the Democrats, a more natural party alliance based on their class and occupations, and weakened their pro-Republican behavior in the voting booth should not be surprising. But the increase in the volume of urban-to-rural migration does seem to imply that a change in the composition of the stream is possible.

In the period before 1960, as the table below shows, the urban-to-rural migration stream was indeed higher in objective social status than any other rural or urban group in the North. In the period after 1960, however, the ranking changed, a clear indication of a shift in the composition of the stream.

Objective Social Status: PDI % High–% Low

	Pre-1960	Post-1960	
urban-rural	− 15	+ 30	stable urban
stable urban	− 20	+ 15	rural-urban
rural-urban	− 31	+ 4	urban-rural
stable rural	− 34	− 35	stable rural

Whereas the overall socioeconomic status of the rural in-migration stream shows an upward trend, relative to other groups it has declined. And based on measures of subjective social class, the rural in-migrants in 1980 are also showing signs of compositional change. In 1970, for example, 55 percent of this movement stream identified with the middle class. This figure dropped to 40 percent in 1980. And when just those who have migrated most recently, within the last five years, are considered, the differences are even more apparent. In 1970, 63 percent of the recent migrants identified with the middle class, whereas in 1980, 33 percent did.

Along with a shift in the social composition of this movement stream, there has been a change in its political traits. In the pre-1960 period, as Table 3.4 shows, urban out-migrants were Republican. After 1960, their partisanship appeared to be more Democratic. This is indicated most clearly by the change in their party identification and their congressional vote. Their presidential vote is also consistent with their movement toward the Democrats.

Finally, people migrating toward rural areas, the pre-1960 cohort in the years after 1964, have drifted toward the Democrats. The explanation for this change is not readily obvious as the aggregate par-

Table 3.4. The Partisan Attributes and Change of Urban to Rural Migrants

	Pre-1960	Post-1960	$\Delta\ t_2 - t_1$ in Pre-1960 Urban to Rural Migrants
Party Identification			
PDI: % Dem – % Rep	− 2	+ 14	+ 8
Congressional Vote			
% Dem	40%	51%	+ 9
Presidential Vote	(1052)	(460)	
% Dem	38%	41%	+ 4
	(909)	(368)	

Source: American National Election Studies, 1952–1980, Center for Political Studies, University of Michigan.

tisan hue of the rural sectors is solidly Republican. And over the years, as shown in Table 3.3, rural areas seem persistently Republican.

Special Instances of Rural-to-Urban Migration

Two historical migration streams deserve special notice. Blacks and whites migrating from the rural South to the industrial centers of the North have been important to national and regional politics since the 1910s. Within both groups those who migrated to the North experienced changes not only from entering an urban world, but also from encounters with a different political culture (Marsh 1967). Overall, their internal migration comes closest to replicating the experience of immigrants (Bernard 1969).

Blacks have made more than one dramatic population movement within the United States. Immediately after the Civil War, large proportions of blacks left the plantation states of Virginia, the Carolinas, and Georgia. Many migrated across the South to the new agricultural regions of Arkansas and Texas. Many more migrated still further south to Louisiana and Florida. And migration out of the Deep South when it did occur was mostly to the contiguous states of the border South. Even though there had been substantial population movement at the turn of the century, 80 percent of all blacks remained rural and southern. From these rural southern beginnings in the United States, by 1980 close to 60 percent of black Americans had become both urban and northern (Hamilton 1964; Piore 1968; Tilly 1967).

The southern out-migration of blacks began in the late 1910s and continued through the late 1940s (Thornbrough 1961). The beginnings of black migration North coincided with the decline of the last great immigration waves from southern Europe. During this time, two million blacks migrated to the North (Taeuber and Taeuber 1958). Like others from rural areas, they migrated in response to the pull of industrial needs, especially for World Wars I and II. Many were also induced to migrate by the collapse of southern agriculture. But for blacks, there were other pushing forces. The political repression that resulted from the Jim Crow laws is a familiar story by now and has no counterpart among whites. The grandfather clause, literacy tests, and the poll tax stripped the blacks of their right to vote and denied them access to public office (Woodward 1967; Mathews and Prothro 1966).

And with these political changes, blacks lost the capacity to gain any social and economic equality through the electoral process. It was just such regressive changes that the Jim Crow laws were designed to promote. When the incessant intimidations and violence directed against blacks by groups like the Ku Klux Klan are also considered, both economic and noneconomic reasons for their exodus from the South seem obvious.

Most demographic data show that the tide of black migration to the North slowed drastically in the depression years after the Second World War (Campbell 1974). The decline of economic opportunities in the North relative to the surge of economic activity within the South and its improving racial climate kept many blacks from migrating. Yet in spite of this decline, for most blacks, even in the 1980s, the south-to-north migrations are important lifelong geographical movement experiences.

Southern Blacks in the Urban North

The composition of the black migration streams out of the South is disturbingly familiar. Among all migrants, blacks have been the poorest, least educated, and the least likely to benefit from geographical mobility. Yet in leaving the South and moving North they were expected to achieve higher levels of education and attain higher incomes than those who stayed in the South.

Living in the rural South had an obvious effect on the social composition of the black migrants. In the pre-1960 period, their socioeconomic standing, even after they had lived in the North, was below that of blacks living either in the North or the South. Among the pre-1960 cohort, there was a modest increase (+14) over time in their objective social status. But with a PDI score equal to -81, they remained well below either the northern or southern general black population.

By 1960, the socioeconomic composition of blacks migrating from the rural South became similar to that of all southern blacks and was well above the level of the pre-1960 stream. Yet even in this later period, blacks exiting the rural South had a social standing far below that of the indigenous blacks in the North.

My interest in black migration is less in the South's political conditions implicated by migration and more in the political effects that black migration had on the politics of the North. Cities like Chicago and New York felt the effect of black voters. In Chicago, the black population grew from 30,000 to 110,000 between 1900 and 1920. In the borough of Manhattan, blacks increased from 2 to 12 percent of the population between 1900 and 1930 (Furniss 1969:21).

Because of their numbers and residential concentration, blacks were quickly drawn into the urban machines. As black participation rates grew, their contribution to a party's electoral success increased dramatically. In the northern cities, as elsewhere, blacks did not gain political power comparable to that of other new urban arrivals (Katznelson 1976). Foreign immigrant groups often lacked language abilities, income, and familiarity with the urban culture, yet they became powerful political elements of the party coalitions typical of urban machines.

The urban world into which blacks migrated was not the same as that of the 1890s or even of the first years of the twentieth century. Major black in-migration to the urban North came precisely at the moment when progressive reforms began to diminish the power of urban machines. While patronage survived into Republican reform administrations, fewer opportunities existed for those who entered politics late. This seemed to be true in industry and commerce as well as in politics (Thernstrom 1964, 1973; Griffen and Griffen 1978; Lieberson 1980). And while it is likely that white nativist feelings might be relaxed to accept leaders or representatives of foreign immigrants in high positions of political power, latent racism and prejudice are not likely to be relaxed when blacks are the group with whom power is to be shared.

It might appear that blacks involved with the urban machines gained personally, but when compared to other ethnic group leaders, few did (Katznelson 1976). And neither did they procure for their group its share of jobs and appointments, the currency of any machine's patron-client system. Early black political elites may have been the ultimate organization leaders. They were not militant on behalf of their group, and they required minimal amounts of patronage in return for black electoral support. The failure of black leaders to provide patronage for their voters may have predetermined their demise. Few survived the revolution in black urban politics which occurred in the late 1960s.

Thus neither the Republicans nor the Democrats in the North fully mobilized blacks prior to 1964 (Petrocik 1980:chap.7). Black voters did not receive any special benefits from the New Deal, and the Republicans failed to take advantage of this weakness in the Democratic coalition.

Even when blacks no longer faced serious legal restriction to political participation, the residue of past Jim Crow laws persisted especially in the South. In the pre-1960s, 19 percent of those blacks living in the South voted and even fewer participated more extensively in politics. Among blacks living in the North at the same time, electoral participation nearly matched the level for whites after socioeconomic differences are considered (Verba and Nie 1972:170). The evidence is shown in Table 3.5.

Blacks who migrated to the North prior to 1960 participated in elections at a rate exceeding those they left behind in the South but at lower rates than those for indigenous northern blacks (Campbell et al. 1960; Marvick 1965). In the years after 1964 when the major impediments to voting and electoral participation were removed, the level of participation rose in the South (Wolfinger and Rosenstone 1980). Yet levels of voting and extra participation remained well below those of blacks who were lifelong residents of the North.

Migrants from the South in the years after 1960 voted and participated at levels similar to those in the South, and again well below those in the receiving area of the North. Yet even in 1980, when the restrictive legal barriers to black participation had been removed for over a decade, black migrants still participated at rates below Northern blacks.

The socioeconomic differences between the indigenous blacks of the North and the migrants from the rural South undoubtedly explain some of the difference in their participation rates. In addition, indigenous urban blacks have a higher level of group consciousness than do black migrants. Black consciousness as a form of generic group identification has been tied repeatedly to higher rates of political participation (Verba and Nie 1972:158). And positive black group consciousness has been found to be relatively weak in southern migrants (Sears and McConahay 1973:chap. 5). Of course, changing the registration and voting laws does not ensure compliance. The bar-

Table 3.5. The Sociopolitical Attributes of Black Groups

	Rural Southern Blacks Migrating to the Urban North		Blacks Living in the South		Blacks Living in the North	
	Pre-1960[a]	Post-1960[b]	Pre-1960[c]	Post-1960[d]	Pre-1960	Post-1960
Objective Social Status						
PDI: % High – % Low	−95 (104)	−67 (29)	−70 (572)	−68 (1023)	−68 (140)	−37 (393)
Party Identification						
PDI: % Dem – % Rep	+53 (101)	+80 (26)	+35 (413)	+66 (984)	+31 (129)	+64 (377)
Congressional Vote						
% Dem	95 (35)	100 (33)	80 (50)	91 (311)	75 (77)	91 (175)
Presidential Vote						
% Dem	80 (40)	nc[e]	54 (89)	93 (298)	75 (47)	95 (123)
Turnout						
% Voting	50 (104)	49 (27)	19 (552)	49 (935)	64 (138)	57 (341)
Extra Participation						
PDI: % Active – % Inactive	−24 (68)	nc	−71 (422)	−22 (539)	−19 (86)	−16 (163)

Source: American National Election Studies, 1952–1980, Center for Political Studies, University of Michigan.
[a]Pre-1960 scores based on pooled 1952 to 1960 NES data for black respondents migrating prior to 1960.
[b]Post-1960 scores based on pooled 1964 to 1980 NES data for black respondents migrating after 1960.
[c]Pre-1960 scores based on pooled 1952 to 1960 NES data for black respondents who were raised and interviewed in the South.
[d]Post-1960 scores based on pooled 1964 to 1980 NES data for black respondents who were raised and interviewed in the South.
[e]Insufficient cases.

riers which are commonly placed in the way of black participation, especially in the South, persist in both blatant and subtle ways.

Partisan directional effects of migration on blacks are also present. After migrating to the North, black citizens became active in the political process and closely tied to the fortunes of the Democratic party. Black migrants in the pre-1960 period and after were more closely linked to the Democratic party than were blacks in the South or lifelong northern blacks, as Table 3.7 shows.

And as Table 3.6 shows, from already high levels of pro-Democratic support, black migrants from the pre-1960 period increased their level of partisan attachment and propensity to vote for the Democrats over time.

Southern Whites in the Urban North

White southerners migrated north as well as west (Brown et al. 1965; Schwarzweller and Brown 1967; Folger 1953; Fairchild 1969). The demographic attributes of white southern out-migrants, like those of blacks, were virtually dictated by their rural and regional background. And like blacks, they have not markedly improved their socioeconomic status after living in the urban North. Whether they came from a farm or a small, rural community, nearly 65 percent of these migrants fall into the lowest level of the Objective Social Status Index. This generalization holds for both the pre- and post-1960 migration streams. After having lived in the North, moreover, the pre-1960 migrants' socioeconomic status remains unchanged.

Despite some similarities, white and black rural southerners who migrated north have ended up with completely different partisan orientations since the 1950s. The partisan composition of the white rural migrants from the South in the years before 1960 was clearly pro-Democratic, based on their party identification difference score (PDI $= +42$). Their voting behavior was also solidly Democratic. Yet this tendency was dramatically reversed after 1960 to strong support for the Republicans (PDI $= -18$). There has also occurred a net decline over time in the pre-1960s cohort's attachment to the Democratic party ($t_2 - t_1 = -24$). This decline in party support is coincident with a drop in the proportion voting Democratic in congressional and presidential races ($t_2 - t_1 = -6$ and -21, respectively). It is important to note that these migrants are in urban centers of comparable size to those that received black migrants from the South.

Indeed, the Republican orientation of the recent white southern out-migrants cannot easily be explained. The white southerners of low socioeconomic status, from whom the out-migrants are drawn,

Table 3.6. Cohort Change in Rural Southern Blacks Living in the North

	Migrant Change[a] $\Delta\ t_2 - t_1$
Objective Social Status	
PDI: % High – % Low	+ 14
Party Identification	
PDI: % Dem – % Rep	+ 27
Congressional Vote	
% Dem	+ 3
Presidential Vote	
% Dem	+ 15
Turnout	
% Voting	+ 11
Participation	
PDI: % Active – % Inactive	+ 10

Source: American National Election Studies, 1952–1980, Center for Political Studies, University of Michigan.
[a]The scores are the difference between post-1960 scores for pre-1960 migrants (t_2) and pre-1960 scores for pre-1960 migrants (t_1).

have been the least likely in the South to switch to the Republicans. It has been the higher status, native white southerners who have declined as a group in support of the Democrats. Again, a closer look at the contextual change is needed to discern the forces acting upon migrants such as these.

Migration to the South

Northerners were migrating south before the term "Sun Belt" was coined. In 1880 over one-half million persons migrated from the North to the South. At that time nearly 2 percent of those born in the North resided south of the Mason-Dixon line. By 1950 over 5 percent of the northern-born population was residing in the South. And this increased to nearly 8 percent in 1970 and 12 percent in 1980 (U.S. Bureau of the Census 1983). The population growth potential of the early north-south migration, however, was lost because of the magnitude of southern out-migration.

Since the 1950s the decline in southern population due to net migration has been reversed. In the early 1970s net migration to the South reached a balance. By 1980 migration favored the South. Since

Table 3.7. Age Migrating by Cross-Regional Migration

	North-to-South		South-to-North	
	1970	1980	1970	1980
Under 25 years	30.6	23.3	48.9	46.9
25–35 years	23.7	31.4	31.1	30.2
Over 36 years	45.8	45.3	20.0	22.9
PDI: % under 25 – % over 35	− 15.2	− 22.0	+ 28.9	+ 24.0

Source: American National Election Study, 1970; American National Election Study, 1980, Pre and Post Election Surveys, Center for Political Studies, University of Michigan.

fewer southerners are leaving, northern in-migration is starting to have an impact on the population growth as well as on the composition of the region (Hauser 1981).

One of the features of the population exchange between the North and the South has been that the composition of the incoming stream is different from that going out. Few illustrations suggest this point better than the age differences between the south-north migrants and the north-south migrants. As Table 3.7 shows, the south-north migrants are younger in that nearly half are under twenty-five years of age. North-south migrants are predominantly over thirty-six years of age. Other analysis, not shown, indicates that social status differences widely separate the two streams as well. Migrants from the North have better educations, are employed in significantly higher status jobs, and enjoy higher incomes than those exiting the South.

There are two distinct groups of north-south migrants. One is made up of retirees who are moving to the sun and retirement centers. The other consists of the northern managers or professionals who have helped usher in the second southern Reconstruction. The political attributes of both groups are important for the effects that they are having on the composition of the region.

High-Status Migrants Moving to the South

Northern in-migration was clearly affecting the level of social class polarization in the South during the 1950s. Converse reported that these migrants were helping bring about a closer relation between occupational status and party which prior to the 1950s had been absent from southern politics. This change in status polarization occurred primarily within the industrializing areas of the South (Converse 1966).

The north-south migrants were Republican. They identified with

Table 3.8. The Political Attributes of High-Status Northern Whites Living in the South

	Migration Stream		Migration Change	High-Status Northerners	
	Pre-1960[a]	Post-1960[b]	$\Delta t_2{}^c - t_1$	Pre-1960	Post-1960
Party Identification					
PDI: % Dem − % Rep	− 20	− 20	−2	− 19	− 11
	(103)	(165)		(1418)	(2664)
Congressional Vote					
% Dem	60%	38%	−9	33%	40%
	(57)	(93)		(1134)	(1781)
Presidential Vote					
% Dem	36%	34%	−1	29%	40%
	(52)	(85)		(925)	(1213)

Source: American National Election Studies, 1952–1980, Center for Political Studies, University of Michigan.
[a]Pre-1960 scores are from the pooled 1952 to 1960 NES data.
[b]Post-1960 scores are from the pooled 1964 to 1980 NES election data for migrants entering their current state after 1960.
[c]The difference between pre-1960 migrants monitored in t_1 (1952 to 1960) and t_2 (1964 to 1980).

the Republican party and voted Republican for presidential candidates. Their curious support of the Democratic party's congressional candidates, as shown in Table 3.8, may reflect the lack of Republican candidates running in the South during this early period. When Republicans began to compete for seats in the South in the early 1960s, these migrants voted for them. Over time, the partisan hue of this group has not changed.

As a group, they can be compared with those of similar socioeconomic status within the North. In the pre-1960 period the migrants exhibited slightly more pro-Democratic tendencies than those remaining in the North. This was true in terms of both their congressional and presidential vote. But among those sampled in the post-1960 period, it has been the northerners who have weakened the staunchness of their Republican support based on their party identification and presidential vote, while the north-south migrants have remained unchanged in their Republican ardor.

The partisan consistency between the pre- and post-1960 movement streams as an indication of the lasting Republican attachment of these migrants is reinforced by the cohort comparisons of the pre-1960 migrants. Over time they have developed even stronger attachments with the Republican party, although not as strong as expected. Based on each measure of partisanship, the north-south migrants have moved in the direction of greater support for the Republican party at relatively slow rates.

It is useful to draw a parallel comparison with another pro-Republican migration stream. Like the north-west migrants, high-status, northern migrants to the South remained Republican but did not further develop their partisan orientation. This fact may be a by-product of the advanced age of the group when migrating. It may also have to do with the nature of the political environments they encountered after migrating, along with their initial support for Democratic congressional candidates. Even in the post-1964 period, half of the pre-1960 migrants voting in such races were Democratic.

Retirees to the South

In an effort to find a community suitable for retirement, yearly a stream of older northerners migrate to the South. In any year approximately 5.6 percent of those of retirement age migrate, and of that, nearly one in five migrate out of the North to the South for the first time. And in the post-World War II period, this trend has steadily increased as greater numbers of those over sixty-five seek the more temperate climate of the South.

Prior to 1960, retirees to the South were largely from the lower socioeconomic strata. As Table 3.9 shows, in this stream 39 percent were more likely to be lower than higher status citizens. Their political orientations do not reflect their social background. While compared to the high-status northerners just discussed, the retirees were more Democratic than Republican. However, their presidential vote and the level of support they gave congressional candidates were less Democratic than for higher status north-south migrants.

The more recent post-1960 stream of retirees are clearly different, but again in a way not easily predicted from their Objective Social Status score (PDI = −22). While they continue to be more drawn from the lower socioeconomic groups, their partisan attributes are solidly Republican. Their party identification and congressional and presidential vote make them one of the strongest pro-Republican groups in the country.

As might be expected, the advanced age of the pre-1960 retired migrants precludes following their cohort over time. If we assume an average age of seventy for the pre-1960 cohort in 1956, they would have been around eighty in the mid-1960s, when the second time span begins. The mortality rate among these advanced age groups is simply too high for any reliable estimate of change. Consequently, we are limited to observing change in the composition of the streams coming into the South over successive years.

Table 3.9. The Sociopolitical Attributes of Retirees Migrating to the South

	Pre-1960[a]	Post-1960[b]
Objective Social Status		
PDI: % High – % Low	− 39	− 22
	(226)	(97)
Party Identification		
PDI: % Dem - % Rep	+ 5	− 34
	(213)	(89)
Congressional Vote		
% Dem	52%	30%
	(164)	(39)
Presidential Vote		
% Dem	34%	23%
	(131)	(38)
Turnout		
% Voting	80%	70%
	(224)	(79)

Source: American National Election Studies, 1952–1980, Center for Political Studies, University of Michigan.
[a]Pre-1960 scores are from the pooled 1952 to 1960 NES data.
[b]Post-1960 scores are from the pooled 1964 to 1980 NES data.

Conclusion

This chapter has mapped the composition of selected population movement streams. It has also attempted in one way to determine whether or not migrants change sociopolitical attributes after migration. The streams selected provide illustrations of migrants with the most dramatic types of movement experience. Most often when we think of those who change their partisan and social environments, it is these migrants we have in mind.

Yet based on the evidence from this chapter, and on a common way of investigating migration effects, it is difficult to draw any definite theoretical conclusion about the effect that generic migration has. But several points are clear. It is highly unlikely that the sociopolitical composition of migration streams themselves are constant over time. It is also unlikely that migrants within the major population movement streams remain politically unchanged after migration. At the same time, it is not possible to assert that migration and what it represents in terms of changing political environments produce significant micropolitical change.

It remains important, however, to have documented the composition and change in these migration streams. They have been important in the past for the rise and decline of various sections of the country. Indeed, hidden in the massive movement streams just outlined, are migration eddies that provide at least the appearance of constancy of population movement. Some places, far removed from one another, appear to swap generations, young parents with their children leaving only to have their grandchildren return to the same villages and towns. There are parts of the Ozarks between southwestern Missouri and northwestern Arkansas that fifty years ago contributed people to the growth of southern California. In the 1970s, their descendants began to return to the Ozarks. But they were different people, more urban, educated, westerners in their language and customs. They returned, however, to become teachers, bankers, and store managers—not rocky hill farmers who supplement meager incomes by hunting, trapping, and making moonshine. The descendants of those early Ozark migrants could have as easily moved to Atlanta, Boston, or Flint. Their movement back to the Ozarks means that population movement streams are probably going to be less distinctive in the future in terms of the people and their sociopolitical qualities.

This chapter has not attempted to analyze the processes by which migration influences the political characteristics of individuals. For this to be done, the type of political environmental change experienced with migration would have to be determined and the political consequences of the environmental change assessed for the individual migrant.

In addition, while the streams discussed are important, even dramatic aspects of the population movement in the United States, they are but a few of the types of relocation that contemporary migrants experience. Again, nearly one-fifth of the population moves every year. And among them, nearly 70 percent migrate across a county boundary. The typical migration described in this chapter, interregional migration, is experienced by only 40 percent of all those who ever move.

In the previous chapter, I showed that the generic quality of migrants, because of the size of internal migration in the United States, tends to be similar to the general attributes of the population. In this chapter geographical disaggregation of the total set of migrants provided visible evidence of their differences depending upon from where they came and to where they moved. For us to fully understand migration and its potential political consequences, the scope of migration should be broadened to include all migrants. Also, the nature of the experience of those moving should be specified to isolate the political quality of migration that appears to influence the political characteristics of migrants. The next chapters turn to the problem of partisan context and contextual change that occurs with internal migration.

Summary

1. The south-to-west migrants were largely from the lower end of
   the objective status hierarchy and associated mainly with the
   Democratic party, both before and after 1960. Moreover, these migrants developed even stronger Democratic ties after migration.
2. The north-to-west migrants came from higher status origin than
   did southern migrants to the West and were less likely to support
   the Democratic party. After migration, northerners in the West
   appeared to experience significant upward social mobility. Yet migration seemed to have eroded the Republican origins of this
   group. Instead of developing solid Republican attributes, they
   tended to adhere to the Democratic party.
3. Northern migrants to the cities and urban areas were drawn from
   the top end of the socioeconomic levels of rural places. Politically
   they were pro-Republican in the pre-1960 era as well as after 1960.
   The composition of the movement stream was at least as Republican as that of those who remained within rural areas and after
   1960 even more so. However, once in the cities, northern ruralites
   moved slowly in a more pro-Democratic direction despite ad-
   vances in their socioeconomic status.
4. The back flow of migration from urban to rural areas has increased steadily over time. The composition of the stream, however, has changed. Prior to 1960, migrants with higher socioeconomic status and pro-Republican tendencies were typical of
   this stream. Over time, the composition has shifted to reflect
   a more working-class, pro-Democratic structure.
5. Black migration from the South has slowed in the last few
   decades. Politically, blacks appear the most likely to be influenced
   by migration. In the pre-1960 period, the level of black migrants'
   turnout and campaign participation increased significantly over
   that of those remaining in the South, though it remained below
   that of those indigenous to the North. Black voters who migrated
   from the South also became strong adherents to the Democratic
   party, a tendency which increased the longer they remained
   in the North.
6. Southern rural whites who migrated North, like blacks from
   the South but unlike whites from the rural North, did not gain in
   terms of socioeconomic status from their trek. They remain one of
   the lower status groups in the urban North. Politically, however,
   they do show a significant shift in political tendencies. In the pre-
   1960 period these migrants were as closely linked to Democratic
   political fortunes as were those who remained in the South. By
   the post-1960 period, like resident southerners, these migrants

began to drift into the Republican camp. This occurred even though their socioeconomic status remained low.

7. North-to-south migrants have included some of the older internal migrants with the highest status. Among this group of professionals and managers, political tendencies have remained steadfast in terms of Republican identifications and voting behavior.

8. A second element in the north-to-south stream is those who move at retirement. While this group is somewhat lower in socioeconomic status than other population movement streams, these migrants nonetheless show increasing tendencies to support and contribute to the growth of the Republican party in the South.

Part II

Political Environments

Chapter 4

Measuring Local Political Environments

Adaptation of migrants to a different political environment cannot be observed if the objective political environmental change is not correctly measured. Previous studies of the effects of migration on politics have failed to distinguish between those migrants whose political environment remained unchanged and those for whom it did change.

Specifying whether geographical mobility occurs within or between regions or communities is not sufficient to determine the political consequences of migration. Even when vast geographical distances are traveled and regional boundaries crossed, migrants may remain within the same type of local political environment. Migration between regions may produce a change in political environment but one not in line with the character of the two regions. For example, a relocation from Cleveland to Dallas may produce a change of political environments from pro-Democratic to pro-Republican. The voter would be introduced to a substantially more Republican political environment, even though it is in the South. Isolating the type of migration experienced in terms of the actual change in political environment may clarify the relation of internal migration to micro politics. Conversely, not considering objective political environmental change may lead to a faulty understanding of the durability and permanence of an individual's core political beliefs.

If we are to understand the political effect of migration, the political environments of the past and the current areas of residence must be measured in as comparable a fashion as possible. And as this chapter shows, contextual analysis is an appropriate technique for determining the political consequences of migration. Assuming that contextual variables have been measured in an unbiased fashion and that the proper statistical techniques have been used, the political behavior and attitudes of migrants can be examined by the types of contexts in which they have lived.

The questions addressed in this chapter step in and out of both theoretical and methodological issues surrounding contextual analysis.[1] What are the components of political environments? Which tend to be the most central to the discussion of environmental change brought on by migration? Can previous and current political environments be measured directly? And if so, when does migration involve a change of political environments? Do migrants move into areas that coincide with their existing political beliefs and partisan loyalties?

Components of Political Environments

For the study of migration, it is important to stress that we must understand both the current local political environment and past local political environments. By a local political environment, I mean the total of all politically relevant events, information, and social interactions that surround an individual. I assume that the local political environment can cause an individual to behave in a way the probability of which is consistent with the information contained in the environment. Certain features of a local political environment seem to be the most critical to this study: personal networks, direct political contacts, and the mass media.

Personal Networks

Personal contacts may be the most casual, flexible, and intimate way in which a local environment can touch an individual (Katz and Lazarsfeld 1955; Lazarsfeld et al. 1948:152). The outcome often involves persuasion without coercion (Lazarsfeld et al. 1948:157). Personal networks may be in physically different places (Cox 1974), and each may affect and be affected by different aspects of an individual's political attributes.

The earliest research on personal contact, mostly conducted at Columbia from the early 1940s to the 1960s, showed that resulting personal networks are different from social groups. They link individuals to others inside and outside of groups to which they belong. For a migrant, social networks could be important for directly transmitting, modifying, or blocking the flow of new political information from the local political environment. The work place, voluntary neighborhood organizations, church, and school may provide situations in which the migrant meets other people face to face. In each case the migrant may be influenced by (or influence) the politics and the political norms of an area. A migrant may learn about the political culture of an area or not, depending on the norms and composition of individuals he or she knows, and the political composition of social group networks.

Whether a migrant adopts political attributes consistent with group norms in a new environment or remains unaffected by a new setting is the question at hand. Depending upon the presence, composition, and role of a personal network, an individual migrant may be either integrated with or insulated from the effects of the external political environment. Resistance to external pressure for change such as community norms or mass media persuasion has been linked with the individual's strength of attachment to primary groups, as well as to the identification with his or her immediate peers (Shils and Janowitz 1948). If a personal contact reflects the surrounding milieu, a migrant might be expected to quickly accept the norms of a place as his or her own. If a salient personal contact or network is antagonistic or indifferent to the surrounding community, a migrant may remain an outsider in the community far longer. As such, personal contacts and group networks within which people live and work can act as pockets of opposition or support. These enable someone to adjust to or fend off dissonant political views, and hence to appear to remain impervious to the external world (R. J. Johnston, letter to the author, Winter 1982).

Direct Political Contacts

Individuals may have two types of direct political contact: contact with a political organization such as a political party, a campaign organization, or an interest group, or contact with an elected official outside the arena of election campaigns.

In assessing the effect of direct party contact as a component of the political environment, we must consider that there are different organizational levels that form the structure of a party. National, state, and local party organizations can overlap one another, especially during an election campaign. By Eldersveld's reasoning, in most parts of the United States there is limited interference in political operations from above or below in a party's organizational hierarchy. As a generic form of an organization, a political party is a stratarchy in which different organizations must tolerate and accommodate one another. Which level of a party organization contributes what proportion of an environment's overall hue may be impossible to unravel, since they often differ from place to place and over time within place (Eldersveld 1982:133). For example, in Chicago political power has been traditionally entrenched at the local level. Wards and precincts tied, to whatever degree, to the city's urban machine are the most salient level of politics in Chicago (Rakove 1975). At times the city's machine has been the most important political entity in the state. Even in cities without powerful patronage-based party machines, community clubs, block volunteer groups, and precinct organizations may give an area its political complexion (Epstein 1958; Wilson 1962; Jewell and Olson 1978). In other places, county, assembly, and congressional district organizations may dominate local politics (Huckshorn 1980). The Westside of Los Angeles, for example, is highly organized around state assembly districts. Personal friendships and electoral arrangements for recruiting and funding liberal Democratic candidates cause these state-mandated political structures to appear nested within a larger political apparatus. The area Democratic organizations end up combining the strength of congressional district campaign organizations and assembly district party organizations with local clubs and city council district political organizations for electoral purposes. The recipients of these coalitional arrangements often extend beyond the local Democratic candidates. Even though these various Democratic organizations cooperate in elections, their character and organization remain separate from the Los Angeles county level political apparatus, and from the state and national party organization.

For a migrant, the direct political contact with a representative of a local political organization is most likely to take place in an election campaign, especially during a national race. During elections there is an increased probability that the migrant will have contact with partisan activists who represent the dominant political strain of the environment. Areas that have a greater concentration of partisans tend to be represented by more organized party activists (Stephens 1981: 181). Not only can these organizations boost turnout, but they can also transmit partisan values in an area as well (Campbell et al. 1960; Katz and Eldersveld 1961; Kramer 1970).

Another type of political organization has evolved recently. Ad hoc candidate organizations and grass roots interest groups are successfully competing with political parties (Crotty and Jacobson 1980). While single issue or special interest groups are associated with new media campaigns, many also organize to work in concert with, independently from, or against an area's political parties. Practically they may present a migrant with a vivid, purely political impression of a place's political environment.

Individual citizens may have direct contact with elected officials or their staffs. In an effort to secure services or assistance with bureaucracies, citizens often initiate contact with elected representatives. Such contacts have been shown to be frequent and to be effective in influencing the vote of those citizens (Cain, Ferejohn, and Fiorina 1984).

Mass Media

The most obvious indicator of the political environment may be the mass media. While party organizations may be the most overtly partisan aspect of the political environment and elected government officials the most persistent, they are often only peripheral to a mass public. Party organizations exist seasonally, and in many places not at all. Further, party organizations in the 1980s are not organized broadly enough to allow uniform contact in most urban areas. Elected officials are often in direct contact with only a small segment of the public.

In the past few decades, increasing amounts of political information have been transmitted by the mass media, but there is little empirical evidence of the political effect of this communication. Most of the early research showed that mass media tend to reinforce and strengthen predispositions rather than change basic political beliefs. The lack of clear effects prompted Klapper (1960) to suggest that citizens seemed to be immune to political messages from the mass media.

For migrants in a new political environment, the electronic and print mass media may play an important role in providing cues about the new community and the local political environment. Determining the media component of the political environment requires knowing which information source is important to the individual and what political information is conveyed and when, as well as the locus of the media. In some states, there may be only one media center, which would be where its effects on the political environment would be monitored. In other places there are overlapping or even nested media sources. And in most places within the United States, national media sources have direct access to local environments.

Finding the effects of mass media on political behavior involves determining both the content of political information transmitted by the mass media and an individual's receptivity or immunity to that information. The issue of an individual's receptivity is treated in the section on selective perception later in the chapter. What is actually transmitted by the media bears directly on its role in contributing to the environmental influence on a migrant's political behavior. Information carried by the mass media usually comes from news services or political campaigns. The effect of news is often assumed to have unintended political effects. Leaving aside whether or not election endorsements influence political behavior for a moment, investigations into the content of television news coverage of political events suggest that it is the flash and dash of campaigns which is often reported. Crowd size or where a candidate is campaigning tend to be covered more than policy issues and the candidate's record (Patterson and McClure 1976; Patterson 1980). Consequently, because tactics and popularity dominate what is broadcast or written up as news, what the public picks up from the mass media is often confined to who is winning or losing the election (Schultz 1983). And within this style of political coverage, Clark and Evans (1983) argue that news media are often biased in slanting coverage toward endorsement of the incumbent.

The importance of new campaign techniques geared to the mass media, such as direct mail and intensive television and radio advertising, is not known. Since many campaigns rely almost completely upon media, there is a changing emphasis from door-to-door campaigns to television in an attempt to reach more people with less effort (Crotty and Jacobson 1980:87).

Political pitches to promote a candidate or a cause or detract from a candidate or a cause may be the most readily available source of a migrant's political information and potential indoctrination. The increased length of campaigns and the vast amounts of money available for many elections may dramatically alter the degree to which these one-way communications come to dominate what people learn about their political environment. Migrants may be a segment of the population especially susceptible to media efforts. They are often uprooted from kinship and primary groups, ties with which would tend to thwart the persuasive appeals of media. When these social ties are broken, an individual may be more vulnerable to pulls and pressures of mass appeals.

Isolating just these three types of interaction and contact with a political environment—personal networks, direct political contacts, and the mass media—is difficult. The components of the political environment are rarely mutually exclusive and jointly exhaustive. Political discussions may be based on the news. Or what was heard in the news from someone else may be passed on in conversations (Sears and Chaffee 1979; Robinson 1976). The mass media may report an activity or policy position of a political candidate. The news may have been received from the local campaign organization as a planned event. Or a candidate may be forced to discuss on a regular basis events reported by the press. Local or regional news sources may report on mass public opinion based on systematic or unsystematic polls. Thus each node of the environment may vary in its relative persuasiveness and partisan content.

Measuring just the components of the current political environment may be a possible, though complex task. But it is surely impossible to cycle back in time, sometimes decades, to measure the migrant's previous environment as defined by personal networks, party organizations, and elements from the mass media. To proceed with the analysis, a summary or proxy measure is needed as a substitute for political environment. An indirect way of understanding and measuring political environment based on proxy measures of past and current political environments must thus be devised.

The Logic of Political Environment

That a change of political environment may affect a migrant's political attributes does not mean that a magical entity exerts an unknown influence. If the environment reflects the average interaction a person has with people or institutions in a place, measuring environmental change experienced when migrating means understanding the environments both before and after a move.

One way of determining the complexion of both the previous and current political environment is areal or geographical context. A local political environment is similar to an ecological niche in biological analysis.[2] Like a physical niche, a local political environment is the sum of all environmental factors acting on an individual. It represents an endogenous process based on the likely average interactions occurring within a bounded space (Erbring and Young 1979; Stipak and Hensler 1982).

A context or local political environment is usually measured as a population average, ratio, or variance within a geographical unit. The unit is representative of the area within which a person lives. A local political environment must be broad enough to include the individual's typical range of political contacts, yet small enough to be politically or socially homogeneous. Political and social contextual variables have been shown to affect political behavior and attitudes (Berelson, Lazarsfeld, and McPhee 1954:93–101; Miller 1956:707–27; Putnam 1966; Butler and Stokes 1976:92–96; Sprague 1973, 1976;

Wright 1977:497–508; Miller 1979:272–73; Brown 1981). While no single areal unit or substantive variables are standard in political behavior analysis, the assumptions about their measurement can be stated.

If the density of partisans is the criteria for the measure of local political environment, the partisans are assumed to be distributed uniformly across the space. Individuals entering an area (in this case migrants) encounter partisans randomly and in proportion to the numerical strength of indigenous partisans.[3] The boundaries of the local political environment are assumed to enclose the most persistent and meaningful political influences for the individual, based on the social interactions and one-way communications likely to occur in a place.

The imprecise meaning of environment and context and the lack of clarity concerning what social mechanism a contextual effect implies have led Hauser and others to discount the utility of any contextual findings (1970, 1974). Hauser was the first of many to point out that contextual effects found in social science research up to as recently as 1970 were given meanings which ranged from the cross-sectional differences between social units, to changes that occur in the composition of group membership over time, to differences between individuals depending upon their group status. The results were often thought to be based on the omission of independent variables, a classic form of a misspecification error, or from self-selection of context of dependent variables presumably explained by the contextual variables (Erbring and Young 1979; Prysby 1976). Several critical reviews concluded that if just the correct individual-level variables were used to explain what people think, feel, or do, then contextual effects would be trivial. The resolution of statistical problems underlying contextual analysis has been treated very well elsewhere (Boyd and Iversen 1979; Alwin 1976:294–303; Sprague 1976; Sprague and Westefield 1979a; Stipak and Hensler 1982).

What is useful here is to point out that a specific social process is assumed to lie beneath the contextual variables monitored. Sprague and Westefield provide a useful way of understanding contextual effects by showing the formal properties of social resonance and political contagion (1979a, 1979b).

In a contained environment, social resonance results from homogeneity of the behavior of a specific group. The higher the degree of homogeneity, the greater the social resonance. The contextual effects are based both on the reinforcing of dominant group norms in the environment and on the projecting of appropriate group behavior to nonmembers.

The process which induces the behavior is social contagion. The greater the frequency of a behavior (within a bounded space), the higher the probability that an individual within the environment will contact those who represent the dominant norms of the area and behave similarly. The assumption of contagion is that the individual can change basic political loyalties, beliefs, and actions permanently as a result of contact.[4]

Proxy Measure of Current and Past Political Environment

We have discussed the meaning and components of past and current political environments, but how can they be measured? I cannot directly measure political environments of the past but instead must find and rely on empirical measures for what I would have found had I begun this study perhaps fifty years ago. Since this analysis could not be done without such a proxy measure, it is necessary to discuss at some length the logic behind the choice of proxy measures of past political environment, the percent voting Democratic in a county during the previous four elections before a person migrated, and why that choice sets limits on the measurement of current political environments.

The political environment in both the previous and current areas is measured by aggregate election results at the county or congressional district level. To the best of my knowledge, this is the only way to determine the local political environments of current and previous areas of residence if comparability of measures and units is to be achieved. Furthermore, the unit of local political environment is also sensitive to the definition of a migration, changing residences by crossing a county boundary, made in Chapter 2.

The partisan nature of the previous political environment is measured by determining the average percentage voting Democratic in the four congressional races prior to the individual's migration. The length of time the individual has lived in the current area is used to refer back to the appropriate year when the last migration occurred.[5]

The current local political environment is measured at two points in time. One point is the time the migrant entered the new area; the second is the time the migrant was interviewed during the election study. For a migrant interviewed in the 1980 NES data who last moved in 1959, the current local political environment is the average percentage voting Democratic in congressional elections in 1974, 1976, 1978, and 1980. The current local political environment at the time of migration is measured forward from the time of migration and includes 1960, 1962, 1964, and 1966.[6]

The level of measurement for the current local political environment is refined using slightly different geographical units. For the current political environment, county or congressional district levels were both employed to obtain a measure more proximate to the individual's likely contacts. In rural areas, where congressional districts often spread across several counties, the county unit is used as a proxy measure of local political environment. In urban areas, the smaller environment tends to be the congressional district. The historical aggregate data available for reconstructing the previous local political environment exists only at the county level.

Reliance on aggregate congressional election data for the construction of the previous and current political environments is subject to a number of constraints. To construct a uniform measure of political environment that matched as much as possible the true, long-term partisan forces to which individuals were exposed, I excluded races for governorship and the U.S. Senate from areal environmental measures. This was largely because of the presence of either short-term disturbances, unacceptably long time periods between races, or noncomparability across states. The time interval between senatorial elections (six years), for example, limits their usefulness for establishing a precise picture of the previous and current context. Data for other statewide elections did not occur with sufficient regularity or were not adequately documented across all states to be useful in a study of national scope.

Aggregate data for presidential elections were collected for each of the past and current residences but were not as useful for the analysis at hand as congressional election data. A considerable amount of experimental work was done to develop measures of local political environment. I experimented with multiple and single year election outcomes from presidential elections alone, from a combination of both congressional and presidential election outcomes, and from congressional elections alone. Aggregate areal measures based on presidential election outcomes were largely unrelated to most micropolitical variables of interest. When a combined presidential and congressional contextual measure was created, it also was not as strongly related to party identification, the congressional vote, or the presidential vote as was a measure of local political environment based solely on four years of congressional election outcomes.

Objective social and economic environmental variables are also not included to map the migrant's past environment. This is not because I feel that social or economic factors do not contribute to the overall composition of an environment. Rather, at the levels of the county, comparable aggregate census measures for education, occupational status, and real disposable income per capita are largely absent prior to 1950. Hence it is not possible to construct reliable aggregate variables for migrants' previous residences. In addition, as is discussed in Appendix C, social and economic contextual variables predicting political variables posit a different process than one which I believe is more appropriate for the political analysis at hand, which focuses on the partisan orientation of the mass public.

Rarely are the physically bounded social environment and the perceived environment analyzed simultaneously, and this study is not one of the exceptions. For some migrants, it is probably true that the relevant environment exists without rigid boundaries, without regard to the relative size of the current objective environment, and is defined solely by social and psychological factors. Yet I do not attempt to estimate directly what migrants perceive their current environment to be, or the amount of environmental change they believe has occurred from their migration. The measurement of environment is independent of the migrant, or even of his or her perceptions.

If a perceived social influence is measurable, it is not in need of a proxy variable. The measures of political environment are both conceived and operationalized as an unmeasurable influence with motionless effects. One would not necessarily expect a normal migrant to be aware of the shift between or within local political environments. At the time of migration and after, politics is probably lower in priority than usual as a migrant worries about settling into a new area. But just because the change is subtle and slow, it does not mean that it does not occur. What constitutes a change of political environments is treated next.

Categories of Political Environmental Change

There are problems, of course, with using political environmental variables for the study of migration. It is not possible to show an effect of political environment on political behavior, partisan loyalties, and policy orientations unless we examine the behavior of individuals who have migrated from one type of local political environment (e.g., Republican) to an environment of a different type (e.g., Democratic). Therefore, either I must follow the same individual for a very long time, which I cannot do, or I must use proxy measures for political environmental change, which I can do. If there is an apparent effect of political environmental change on individual political behavior, other theories that if true might have resulted in the same behavioral or attitudinal change must also be examined. As

Table 4.1. Partisan Contextual Change: Categorical Change in Political Context by Partisan Concentration

	Previous Partisan Context		
	Republican[a]	Competitive[b]	Democratic[c]
Current Partisan Context			
Republican[a]	Congruent	Mixed	Incongruent
Competitive[b]		Pure Competitive	
Democratic[c]	Incongruent	Mixed	Congruent

⬜ Migrated within or toward a pro-Democratic environment.

◧ Migrated within or toward a pro-Republican environment.

[a]A Republican environment is defined as one with less than 45 percent voting for the Democratic congressional candidates.
[b]A competitive environment is defined as one where between 46 and 54 percent of the area votes for the Democratic congressional candidates.
[c]A Democratic environment is defined as one where at least 55 percent vote for the Democratic congressional candidates.

pointed out above, there is a literature which notes special caution and problems with environmental and contextual analysis. There is as well a literature which argues that migration does not have much influence on individual political behavior. Addressing both sets of alternative explanations will depend on successfully measuring political environmental change.

There are three sorts of change of environment a migrant could experience: congruent, incongruent, and something in between. This classification, as shown in Table 4.1, relies upon the migrant's being exposed to some type of dominant partisan environment in either the previous or the current area. A *congruent* migration occurs when movement is within the same type of political environment. An *incongruent* migration is a change in the political environment. Operationally an incongruent migration is defined as a move from a local environment dominated by one party to an environment dominated by an opposition party or to a highly competitive political environment. In both instances the homogeneity of the previous local environment is broken by migration. Such experiences are the logical antithesis of a congruent migration, because relocation crosses partisan boundaries. The final type of environmental change, labeled *mixed*, occurs when, after migration, the new political environment neither contradicts nor reinforces the previous environment. Migration from a highly competitive setting to one dominated by a party represents neither a congruent nor an incongruent migration. Living in a long-term competitive environment means that the frequency and intensity of the communications from the parties and the candidates to the individual must be fairly well matched if the competitive situation is to be maintained. Presumably the contact with partisans from the dominant parties within such a competitive environment is also matched. When migrating from such a local political environment to one where only one party dominates, the individual has a better chance than do incongruent migrants of eventually reflecting the partisan attributes of the current environment.[7] Mixed migrants' experience in their previous competitive local environment also implies that the influence of the current local environment will not be as reinforcing as it is for congruent migrants.

A move also has a definite partisan ring, a Democratic tone or a Republican tone. The following chapters separate out those who have stayed within or moved toward a more Democratic environment from those who have stayed within or moved toward a more Republican setting.

Based on a sample of categorical measure of change, over half of all migrants in 1980, even including the South, experienced incongruent or mixed migration. And this proportion increases by about 10 percent when migrations within the South or from the South to the North are removed from consideration, or when the definition of what constitutes a change of political environments is weakened. Approximately 39 percent of all migrants experienced congruent migrations. Forty-four percent stayed within the same general type of local political environment if competitive-to-competitive migrations are counted with partisan congruent migration. Table 4.2 shows the distribution for migrants' contextual change based on the 1980 NES data.[8]

Debunking Self-Selection

The effects of political environments on individual political behavior would be spurious if migrants self-select areas by their political preferences. In operational terms, self-selection would occur if the partisan attributes of migrants at the time of the move match the political environment of the receiving area. Among Americans, partisan considerations are currently not a consideration in a decision to migrate (Sell 1983). However, a subtle form of partisan self-selection might occur. Who would not agree that higher income migrants

Table 4.2. Percent Distribution of Migrants' Contextual Experience between Current and Previous Contexts

| | Previous Partisan Context | | | |
	Republican[a]	Competitive[b]	Democratic[c]	Total
Current Partisan Context				
Republican	14.5[d]	9.6	12.1	36.2
	(117)	(78)	(98)	(293)
Competitive	4.7	4.8	5.9	15.5
	(38)	(39)	(48)	(125)
Democratic	12.0	11.4	25.0	48.3
	(97)	(92)	(202)	(391)
Total	31.1	25.8	43.0	100
	(252)	(209)	(348)	(809)

Source: American National Election Study, 1980, Pre and Post Election Surveys, Center for Political Studies, University of Michigan.

[a] A Republican environment is defined as one with less than 45 percent voting for the Democratic congressional candidates.

[b] A competitive environment is defined as one where between 46 and 54 percent of the area votes for the Democratic congressional candidates.

[c] A Democratic environment is defined as one where at least 55 percent vote for the Democratic congressional candidates.

[d] Cells are total percentages, *N*'s are in parentheses.

move to wealthier neighborhoods, or that white-collar and professional migrants move into different areas from those settled by unskilled migrants? Yet even if this does occur at the neighborhood level, it does not appear to produce *political* side effects for larger areas of aggregation such as the county or congressional district.

One way to determine the degree of partisan self-selection is to examine the correlations between an individual's party identification at the time of migration and the political environment in the previous and the current area. To minimize the confusion between selectivity and the adaptation that may occur after migration, only those who have migrated within five years prior to being interviewed are used in this test. Those within five years of having migrated should have had the least exposure to the political forces of the current environment. Recent migrants are also likely to possess political characteristics held prior to migration.

The evidence as presented in Table 4.3 shows the correlation between migrants' party identification by the previous and current local political environments within the first five years after migration. The correlations are shown for both all recent migrants (those moving within the last five years) and recent migrants moving only

Table 4.3. Partisan Self-Selection among Recent Migrants

	1970		1980	
	Total	Non-South	Total	Non-South
Political Environment				
Previous	.058[a]	− .103	− .089	− .071
	(443)	(248)	(439)	(265)
Current at Time of Migration	.014	.004	− .061	.052
	(293)	(152)	(361)	(199)

Source: American National Election Study, 1970; American National Election Study, 1980, Pre and Post Election Surveys, Center for Political Studies, University of Michigan.
[a]Cell entry is the Pearson *r* correlation between recent migrant's partisan identification and the political environment.

within the non-South. The data are taken from two sources, the 1970 and the 1980 NES surveys. Seven out of eight of the correlations are not significantly different from zero. And the only significant correlation has the wrong sign.

In this way, migrants neither exit nor enter areas on the basis of partisan concentrations. It appears that partisan self-selection is not associated with migration. Thus for the purposes of this study, the partisan political environmental change associated with migration can be tested for the effects it may have on citizens' political attributes without concern about self-selection biases.

Summary

1. Local political environments are the sum of all external social interactions and one-way communications that influence a migrant. The components of the local political environment include personal contacts, direct contacts with elected officials and parties, and the mass media.
2. The meaning of context depends upon the social process operating within the political environment. We assume social contagion.
3. Election outcomes aggregated at the county or congressional district level are a useful way of estimating political environment. Environmental variables are calculated using the average outcome of four congressional elections aggregated at the county (or congressional district) level for past and current environments.
4. A change of local political environments is measured by geographical contexts for both the previous and the current environ-

ments. From the perspective of the current political environment, migrations can be congruent, incongruent, or mixed with reference to a previous political environment.

5. Self-selection of current political environment does not appear to occur.

Chapter 5

Neutralizing Partisanship

"But that," said Perion, "is nonsense." "Of course, it is," said Horvendile. "That is probably why it happens."

—James Branch Cabell, *Jurgen*

This chapter looks at how a migrant's partisan identification, presidential and congressional voting behavior, and psychological and behavioral measures of political commitments are influenced by previous and current local political environments. When migration causes a person to change political environments, his or her partisan attitudes and actions may be altered. When migration does not coincide with a change of political environments, there will be little change in the pattern of past political behavior or political beliefs.

The effect of local political environments should be most evident for migrants' voting behavior. As an individual partisan attribute, voting behavior responds more than party identification to short-term pressures for change. In both Europe and in the United States, individuals show a greater tendency to shift their vote than to shift their party identification in the face of partisan forces (Budge, Crew, and Farlie 1976; for an opposite view, see Thomassen 1976). On the other hand, an individual's party identification tends to be very stable over time and remains so even when a citizen votes for candidates other than those in his chosen party. Party identification also has been shown to persist across generations (Jennings and Niemi 1981:chap. 4). Repeated electoral defections such as might be expected for individuals who migrate into different political environments may eventually erode their underlying party loyalties. A shift in a migrant's party identification would also suggest that the nature of micropolitical change associated with migration is permanent. It would elevate migration to a rather unique status among demographic attributes and call into question previous findings that show no individual-level effect of population movement. As such, voting behavior and party identification are excellent sets of variables to use in studying the micropolitical effects of political environmental change brought on by migrating.

Effects of Changing Local Political Environment

The previous chapter discussed the operational definition of movement within and across local political environments. The analysis that follows builds off of the categorical definition of congruent, incongruent, and mixed political migrations by describing the partisan attributes of migrants. Migrants are first described in terms of their party identification, congressional vote, and presidential vote by the type of political environmental change they experience with migration. The subsequent analysis elaborates the effect on the long-term component of the vote, party identification.

Past evidence showed no general individual political effects of migration. Even when migrants were assumed to have experienced a change of local political environment, there were no effects of the new political environment. Evidence presented in Table 5.1 shows that when local political environment is considered, migrants' partisan attributes differ substantially on the basis of their past and current local political environments.

Among persons migrating toward a Democratic environment from a Republican environment, 58 percent voted Democratic in congressional races as compared to 32 percent who moved within Republican environments. A similar difference, 52 percent and 29 percent, respectively, holds for the 1980 presidential vote. Differences also occur in the migrant's party identification: 41 percent of those who migrated out of Republican environments and into Democratic strongholds identified with the Democratic party as compared to only 23 percent of those migrating within Republican contexts.

Among incongruent migrants who crossed to a Republican environment from a Democratic environment, 23 percent voted Democratic in congressional races as compared to 85 percent of the congruent migrants who did not leave a Democratic environment. Presidential vote and party identification also respond to the effect of changed local political environments. Only 29 percent of congruent

Table 5.1. Migrant and Nonmigrant Micropartisan Attributes by Partisan Contextual Change

		Previous Partisan Context											
		Republican[a]			Competitive[b]			Democratic[c]			Nonmigrants		
		PI	CV	PV	PI	CV	PV	PI	CV	PV	PI	CV	PV
Current Partisan Context	Republican	23[d] (113)	32 (63)	29 (66)	31 (76)	24 (47)	24 (47)	36 (73)	23 (43)	29 (51)	24 (73)	23 (43)	31 (51)
	Competitive	33 (38)	53 (21)	35 (24)	35 (39)	40 (25)	32 (32)	35 (45)	46 (25)	36 (27)	41 (33)	65 (20)	33 (18)
	Democratic	41 (97)	58 (55)	52 (60)	37 (88)	67 (48)	40 (54)	52 (198)	85 (98)	50 (112)	54 (110)	79 (107)	51 (130)

Source: American National Election Study, 1980, Pre and Post Election Surveys, Center for Political Studies, University of Michigan.
[a] A Republican context is defined as one with less than 45 percent voting for the Democratic congressional candidates.
[b] A competitive context is defined as one where between 46 and 54 percent of the area votes for the Democratic congressional candidates.
[c] A Democratic context is defines as one where at least 55 percent votes for the Democratic congressional candidates.
[d] Cells are in percent Democratic. Party identification (PI) is the percent strong plus weak Democratic; congressional vote (CV) is percent voting for a Democratic candidate; presidential vote (PV) is percent voting for Carter.

migrants who remained within a Republican milieu voted Democratic in the presidential contest compared to half of those migrating between a Republican and a Democratic setting. Likewise, over half of the incongruent migrants who shifted from a Republican- to a Democratic-dominated area identified themselves as Democratic partisans compared to only 36 percent of the congruent migrants who moved within Republican environments.

Congruent migration appears to leave the individual migrant a stronger partisan in terms of vote and party identification, especially in comparison to incongruent migrants. In the absence of objective political change in local milieu, the individual migrant experiences a continuity of homogeneous political cues and feels and acts as a steadfast, loyal partisan.

One way to further explore the political consequence of migrating within and across political environments is to look at those who do not migrate at all. Nonmigrants, those who have lived in the same county all of their life, can also be classified according to the nature of their local political environment. As such, they represent a unique group that can act as a benchmark to compare to congruent and incongruent migrants.

There are significant differences between the congressional and presidential votes of incongruent migrants and the votes of those they left behind. Among nonmigrants within local Republican environments, 23 percent voted for Democratic congressional candidates and 31 percent voted Democratic in the presidential contest. Incongruent migrants who left Republican strongholds for Democratic-dominated environments are by comparison far more Democratic. Their votes were 58 percent and 52 percent Democratic for congressional and presidential candidates respectively. As to the party identification of incongruent migrants and nonmigrants, 34 percent of the nonmigrants within Republican environments identified themselves as Democrats compared to 41 percent of those who moved from Republican to Democratic areas.

For the Democratic side a similar set of differences exists. Among nonmigrants within Democratic environments, 79 percent voted Democratic in congressional races, 51 percent voted for Carter, and 54 percent identified themselves as Democratic partisans. By comparison, incongruent migrants who exited Democratic areas were more similar to lifelong residents of Republican areas.

A mixed change in local political environment produces effects consistent with the pull of the current environment. A mixed change of environments is one where the migrant moves from a highly competitive to a party-dominated environment. Table 5.1 also shows a comparison between migrants who remained within politically competitive areas, in the center cell, and migrants who left competitive environments for settings dominated by a single political party. Again, the pull of the current environment on their voting behavior is evident. Only 24 percent of the migrants who left competitive environments and moved to Republican areas supported the Democratic congressional candidate, compared to 67 percent of those who left competitive settings and entered Democratic areas. A similar pattern can be observed for presidential voting behavior. Those who moved to local environments with a dominant partisan coloration shifted their vote in a fashion consistent with the current environment. For mixed migrants, shifts in party identification are again consistent with the partisan concentration of the current political environment, with the caveat that the shift is far less pronounced than that for incongruent migrants.

Adjusted Vote

While partisan self-selection does not occur with migration, social or economic self-selection by area probably does. When socioeconomic self-selection occurs, it may contribute, indirectly, to spurious association between a migrant's political attributes and the political environmental change experienced with a move. To ensure that the effects reported in the previous section are correct, a series of linear corrections of the congressional and presidential vote variables and party identification are performed to control out the potential biasing effects of migrants' social and economic attributes. Specifically, the disturbing effects of a variety of socioeconomic attributes of socioeconomic status and mobility, subjective social class, family income, and education are removed prior to the estimation of the relationship between vote and partisan environmental change.

It should be pointed out that in the adjustment procedures there is no effort to fully specify a model of either the congressional or presidential vote. For example, a model of congressional vote would surely include whether or not the candidate was an incumbent, what specific services the candidate performed for the respondent or other persons the respondent knows in the district, measures of the respondent's perceived performance of the candidate, and the individual voter's party identification (Jacobson and Kernell 1981:16; Kiewiet 1983:102–8). In not doing so, I implicitly acknowledge, as was suggested in Chapter 1, that it is precisely many of these political processes working at the local level that make up the local political environment.[1]

The net effects of changing partisan environments on the 1980 congressional and presidential votes are presented in Figures 5.1 and 5.2. The percentage differences between the expected and the observed proportion of the Democratic vote totals have been presented across the categories of political environmental change. Difference scores greater than zero indicate that the expected proportion voting Republican was higher than the observed Republican vote and that, consequently, the net effect within the environmental change category was to pull migrants in the direction of the Republican party's candidate. Entries of less than zero indicate that the observed proportion voting Democratic was greater than expected, and therefore that the pull of the environmental forces was to the benefit of the Democratic candidate: more Democratic votes were received than would normally be expected on the basis of the migrant's socioeconomic status and partisanship. Finally, the political nature of the local environment in the current place of residence is highlighted as movement toward or within a pro-Democratic or pro-Republican area.

Even after the impact of socioeconomic factors and party identification are statistically removed, migration across a political environment affects an individual's vote. The average net adjustment of the congressional vote in response to a categorical shift in partisan environment is approximately 10 percent when the migration is toward or within a pro-Republican context, 15 percent when migration is toward or within a pro-Democratic context. For the presidential vote, the average net effects are 13 percent and 16 percent for Republican and Democratic contexts respectively. This supports the previous finding that partisan environmental change has significant effects on the voting behavior of migrants (Brown 1981).

Asymmetrical Pull of Partisan Environments

What is also found is a clear asymmetry between the pull of current Democratic and Republican environments. In earlier work (Brown 1981), using only the 1970 NES data, I initially suspected that the asymmetry was the result of the unique regional quality of some Democratic areas. A third of all internal migration takes place within the South. Southern politically congruent migrants often move within highly Democratic local environments. The local political en-

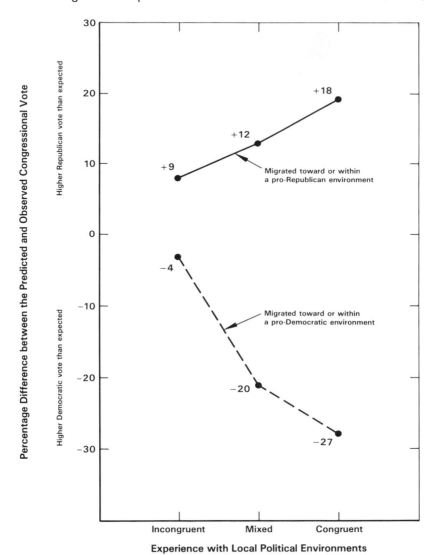

Figure 5.1

Actual Minus Adjusted 1980 Congressional Vote
by Local Political Environmental Change

Source: American National Election Study, 1980, Pre and Post Election
Surveys, Center for Political Studies, University of Michigan.

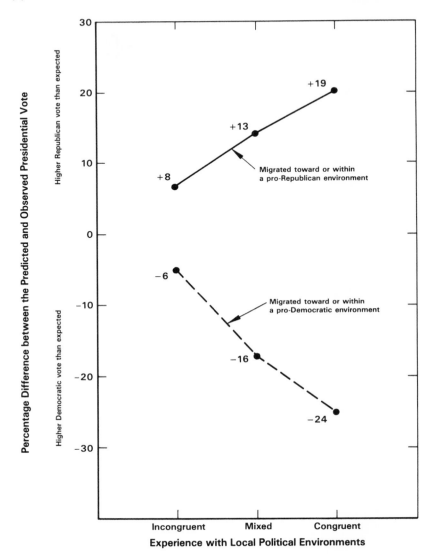

Figure 5.2

Actual Minus Adjusted 1980 Presidential Vote
by Local Political Environmental Change

Source: American National Election Study, 1980, Pre and Post Election
Surveys, Center for Political Studies, University of Michigan.

vironments in the South may have a far greater density of Democrats than is found in other dominant environments outside the South. Congruent migration within Democratic environments in the South when averaged with the overall national patterns of migration may distort the relative estimate of the influence of Democratic environments. In my previous analysis, statistical adjustments including both regional and socioeconomic variables accounted for all of the zero-order differences between the effect of Democratic and Republican political environments on the congressional vote (Brown 1981). In the current analysis using 1980 NES data, the asymmetry, though not great, persists even when exogenous variables, region and socioeconomic factors, are considered. Democratic environments, relative to Republican environments, show a stronger pull on the congruent migrant's vote. Republican environments, on the other hand, have a greater effect on an incongruent migrant's vote.

At this time, I can only speculate why this asymmetry has appeared. Part of the story may be that within Republican-dominated areas, the Republican party has a greater draw on Democrats now than in the past. In the early 1980s, the Republicans relied more heavily on high technology in every aspect of election campaigning, from fund raising to research, than did the Democrats. Only recently have the Democrats attempted to build party resources that take advantage of new technology. Mailing lists of potential contributors, media centers accessible to local candidates, and training facilities for candidates and their staff were simply not available through the Democratic party earlier in the decade. Democrats still lag far behind in the use of advanced research techniques for conducting campaigns, let alone in the training of candidates and campaign staff for effective local organization. Republicans are thus able to offer candidates greater political services and financial support, and those advantages are aimed at vulnerable Democrats, which incongruent migrants clearly are.

Within and outside of the South, Democratic environments continue to show strong pulling effects on their own partisans. Why? Part of the answer may be that the Democratic party has always relied more on ancillary organizations to push voter involvement and to insure a reasonable turnout, the key to Democratic election victories. Congruent migration within Democratic environments may involve more movement within voluntary organizations, social groups, and churches and temples—all of which provide an added Democratic influence.

In summarizing this point, contrary to past research, the current local political environment does play an important role in influencing the presidential and congressional vote of migrants. For politically congruent migrants, their current political environment appears to reinforce the previous political environment. Incongruent migrants appear to have their votes changed by prolonged exposure to different local political forces. The vote of incongruent migrants falls midway between the expected or normal vote of their current and previous political environments. In the aggregate, the voting behavior of incongruent migrants seems to adapt to their new area. Also the shadow of their past experiences in a different milieu is evident. The joint effects of previous and current environmental experiences are evident whether incongruent migrants enter or exit Democratic or Republican areas. This joint effect of both previous and current environments is present for incongruent migrants' congressional and presidential votes.

An aggregate group process may be a misleading indication of how individual migrants behave or think politically. A vote is an either/or behavior. A voter does not vote midway between two parties' candidates. The aggregate evidence indicates that more than half of the incongruent migrants change their vote to match the political tendencies of the new area. Again, the assumption is that this shift would not have occurred if the migration had been congruent or if the individual had stayed within his or her previous environment. Even in the face of a very clearly different partisan environment, many incongruent migrants remain impervious to the political tendencies of their new environment, despite what we must assume is repeated exposure to partisan cues in an overwhelmingly one-sided area. Some of the reasons for this behavior are taken up in Chapter 6.

Adjusted Party Identification

It cannot be determined by just observing migrants' voting behavior whether a change of partisan local environments induces shifts in their basic political loyalties. Nor can it be determined from examining the vote if the steadfastness among congruent or some incongruent migrants is the product of sustained loyalty or simply the result of their not perceiving the objective change of political environments.

If the migrant's congressional or presidential vote does not respond to environmental change, other stable, more basic, partisan attributes such as party identification would probably also not respond. But as Table 5.2 suggests, partisan attitudinal measures appear to shift with a change in partisan environment.

Why should party identification be influenced by environmental change? In the United States, people change their vote in congressional elections without changing their party identification. An election forces action; it takes place in the midst of a campaign which focuses attention on the candidates and issues of the day. For example, in strong Republican areas Republican candidates speak to largely Republican audiences, distribute Republican literature, enjoy the support of the mass media, and generally provide the short-term partisan forces operating on the electorate. Indeed, congressmen may have an additional edge because the services they perform for their constituents are given regardless of the voter's party loyalties. Further, they appear to have some impact on the outcomes (Mayhew 1974; Fiorina 1977; Krehbiel and Wright 1983).

Increasingly, the vote for congressional candidates and the presidential vote have been separate and disjoint. Coattail effects of a successful president once provided a considerable draw for congressional candidates of the president's party. This effect has diminished over time (Calvert and Ferejohn 1983). The decision to vote for a congressional candidate seems to be linked to local rather than national concerns and to the efficacy of a local campaign rather than a national campaign. In addition, there are other factors, like incumbency, that lead the citizen to support the locally dominant party. What effect such a change in the structural ties between votes at different levels of government has on the party loyalty of voters is not clear. Factors that show both the congressional and presidential vote moving together may ultimately be influencing the individual voter's general partisan beliefs. Incongruent migration between local political environments seems to fit this bill rather well.

Migration has been used to show the immunizing effect that party identification can have. Yet little has been said about the role that geographical mobility may play in developing partisan loyalty. When the congruence or incongruence of partisan contextual experience is considered, geographical mobility appears to have a role in forging and changing party loyalties, especially if people become committed to actions they already perform. As Stinchombe suggests, "One way to socialize people is to get them to act . . . and to allow belief to follow" (Stinchcombe, 1975).

The party identification of migrants seems to fit the expectations of some form of political adaptation. Incongruent and congruent changes in political environment that persist produce systematic differences in the party identification of migrants. As the evidence in Table 5.2 shows, congruent migrants who have continual exposure to Republican environments identify more with the Republican party than do incongruent migrants living within comparable environ-

Table 5.2. Mean Party Identification by Change of Partisan Context

Migration Toward or Within:	Incongruent		Mixed		Congruent	
	Total[a]	>11 Years	Total	>11 Years	Total	>11 Years
Pro-Republican Context (N)	2.63 (73)	2.31 (48)	2.92 (65)	2.75 (41)	3.36 (95)	3.46 (47)
Pro-Democratic Context (N)	2.65 (75)	2.37 (64)	2.32 (37)	2.22 (36)	2.43 (71)	1.86 (84)
Mean Difference	−.02	−.06	.60	.53	.93	1.60
Adjusted Mean Difference[c]	−.09	−.02	.31	.24	.90	1.10

Source: American National Election Study, 1980, Pre and Post Election Surveys, Center for Political Studies, University of Michigan.
[a]The total cell entry is the mean party identification scored in the standard fashion: strong Democrats = 0; weak Democrats = 1; independent Democrats = 2; independent Republicans = 3; independent Republicans = 4; weak Republicans = 5; strong Republicans = 6.
[b]The cell >11 years is for those migrants residing in their current community for eleven years or more.
[c]The party identification scores adjust for the migrants' socioeconomic, age, and demographic factors.

ments or congruent migrants who have stayed within Democratic areas. Congruent migrants who have been continually exposed to strong Democratic forces at the local level, in spite of their geographical mobility, develop strong attachments to the Democratic party especially in comparison to migrants with exposure to different political environments.

Incongruent migrants only partially swing their party identification to match the political environmental forces of the current area. The result of this partial adaptation is that these migrants end up looking much like political independents. The party identification of incongruent migrants, therefore, is not significantly distinguishable based on the nature of their local political environments. Incongruent migrants entering pro-Democratic environments identify with political parties in much the same way as those entering pro-Republican environments. While incongruent migrants are neither different from one another nor different from political independents, they are different from congruent migrants. Again, it is assumed that incongruent migrants would have identified with political parties differently if they had moved to politically similar places.

An individual's party identification might not respond quickly to the rather gross differences in local political environment. The partisan cues of the new environment may take a long time to influence the migrant. If attitudinal adjustment occurs after migration, those exposed to the current political environment for the longest period of time should show the greatest effect.

As Chapter 4 shows, among the most recent migrants there is no correlation between partisan environmental change and party identification. And when recent and earlier migrants are combined in a single analysis, as in Table 5.2, decoding the full amount of change may be difficult. But if a set of migrants who have lived in an area a long time show a congruence between their political party loyalty and their local political environment even when their socioeconomic and demographic differences are considered, the congruence of local political environmental change experienced with migration may be an important element in the development, maintenance, and change of an individual's political orientation.

Table 5.2 also shows migrants who had a minimum of eleven years in their current political environment. This is not an arbitrary cutoff point. In this period of time a migrant has been exposed to five congressional elections and two presidential election campaigns. The partisan nature of the immediate political environment would be hard to miss. It is assumed that eleven years is a sufficient period for migrants to show adaptation to the current environment. In addition, around eleven years is the period of time needed for the social uprooting effects of migration to diminish, and for the individual to approach the level of life satisfaction, personal competence, and political efficacy of the stable population (Brown 1987).

Migrants appear to develop a party identification over time that follows the direction of their overall partisan environmental experiences. Over time the party identification of migrants sorts out those who had congruent migrations rather nicely. Congruent migrants moving within Democratic or Republican local environments develop strong party identifications that reflect the partisan tendencies of their surrounding communities. Even when the party identification of congruent migrants is adjusted for their differences in socioeconomic status, region, and age, those who move within comparable local political environments develop strong party loyalties that mirror their environmental experiences. For congruent migrants, partisanship appears to develop as though no geographical move had occurred.[2]

The difference in adjusted mean party identification scores shows that the micropolitical consequences of congruent and incongruent migration persist even when the effects of age, socioeconomic standing, and region are considered. Incongruent migrants are different from congruent migrants in terms of their party identification. Locked between the more extreme partisan loyalties of strong identifiers, incongruent migrants change over time toward political independence by moving toward the center of the party identification continuum. Regardless of the party tendency dominating their local political environment, incongruent migrants stay indistinguishable from each other.

Depending upon the type of migration experienced—mixed or incongruent—individuals who change partisan environments appear to have their party identification stunted by migration. For some, of course, there is no abandonment of earlier political experiences. Many may have been too young at the time of their migration for a psychological attachment to party to have solidified. But for many, migration represents an important point of change in their political lives. If the draw of place happens to put a person in a setting comparable to that prior to migration, the individual develops a rather robust sense of political self. If the move places the individual in a politically different environment, however, often the individual does not develop a strong party attachment.

If partisan loyalty depends on a continuous process of learning and reinforcement throughout life, and not just on childhood experiences, migration across partisan environments operates like a wild card on the individual's political life. It may interrupt the normal process of development and attenuate the individual's ties to partisan politics.

That incongruent migrants end up without a party identification, or possessing a weakened sense of party loyalty, may be a result of the generalized decrease in their level of political commitment. In Table 5.3 the level of political commitment by environmental change is examined directly. Strength of party identification, psychological involvement in politics, efforts made to persuade others to vote in certain ways, and actual reported turnout are used to measure different facets of political commitment. To examine the developmental qualities of political commitment just discussed, evidence is also shown for migrants living eleven years or more in their current political environment.

Surprisingly, there are scant differences in the level of political commitment for the total set of all migrants, even when their experiences with local political environment are considered. Congruent and incongruent migrants who have lived in a place for at least eleven years, however, do show clear differences for the strength of party identification and turnout. Among incongruent migrants, the strength of their party commitment and their propensity to vote is lower than for congruent migration. Moreover, congruent migrants appear to develop a stronger attachment to party and vote at increased rates over time. A similar drop-off in levels of political commitment occurs for those exiting highly competitive environments, mixed migrants, if they are compared to those migrating from one competitive setting to another. The other measures of political commitment do not show clear patterns of differences by type of political environmental change.

The pattern of data shown in Table 5.3 is consistent with the expectation that an uninterrupted local political environment reinforces and consequently strengthens the individual's level of political commitment. Conversely, breaking the flow of information and changing the type of contact in the local political environment disrupts the development of overall political commitment.

The response of individual migrants to a change of political environments seems similar to the social judgment process in that individuals could average new information into rather than add it to existing belief systems. Cognitive addition differs from cognitive averaging in the following way. Under conditions of cognitive addition, an individual with a very strong set of political predispositions, such as a strongly held partisanship, would have those beliefs strengthened, even if a little, by experiences, events, or people who are judged positively. The positive reaction adds to the previous

Table 5.3. Migrants' Level of Political Commitment by Partisan Contextual Change

			Previous Partisan Context											
			Republican[a]				Competitive				Democratic			
			SPI[b]	PSY	INF	T	SPI	PSY	INF	T	SPI	PSY	INF	T
Current Partisan Context	Republican	Total	62	18	25	69	57	24	22	72	61	23	36	73
		>11 Years	81	21	27	85	54	30	20	71	48	12	32	73
	Competitive	Total	63	22	30	68	80	55	32	100	45	NA	14	60
		>11 Years	65	25	25	67	77	39	17	100	44	NA	12	75
	Democratic	Total	63	21	32	74	54	17	19	69	60	21	33	71
		>11 Years	63	23	39	75	67	17	16	61	81	27	27	82

Source: American National Election Study, 1980, Pre and Post Election Surveys, Center for Political Studies, University of Michigan.
[a]See Table 5.1 for heading definitions.
[b]SPI = % having partisan identification; PSY = % high psychological involvement; INF = % persuading others how to vote; T = % voting in last election.

positive attitudes, in this case strongly held partisan predispositions. Democratic partisans who move to a place where the political environment reflects less than a majority, say 45 percent Democratic, would still have their partisanship strengthened. In the strongest bastions of the Republican party there are some Democrats. A cognitive averaging process, however, would weaken rather than strengthen an individual's partisanship under exactly the same conditions. Under cognitive averaging, new information containing weaker cues, such as those coming from an incongruent political environment, is averaged into those of the previous environment. Averaging political information from a new environment with that of the prior environment would result in a weakened party identification and a lower commitment to politics. For congruent migrants, cognitive addition seems to explain their response to migration. On the other hand, an averaging process appears at work among incongruent migrants, given their response to environmental change in terms of their partisan identification and political commitment.

Conclusion

Migrants do not cross political boundaries to change their basic political orientations. Yet in a game with nature, irrespective of the starting political environment and the implicit strategic neutrality of context, a citizen who migrates can evolve in a curious way. When internal migration reinforces a partisan context, the micropolitical effects of migration are of little lasting consequence. Partisan congruence between past and current environments allows for an uninterrupted development of strong partisan attitudes and consistent actions. But when migration places the person in a different environment, the full development of partisanship is seriously altered in the direction of the dominant partisan forces of the current milieu. Over time, incongruent migrants increasingly think of themselves as nonpartisans or weaker partisans, while their voting behavior mimics that of the dominant party in the host area. Incongruent migrants appear to move toward positions of both partisan alignment in their behavior and partisan neutrality in their attitudes.

One could dismiss the findings reported here. The indicators used to measure political environment are very robust and blunt and consequently miss many of the subtle effects of local politics. Environmental change in terms of numerical concentration and density of Democrats and Republicans also does not touch upon the consequences associated with changing communities, homes, friendships, and occupations that are always part of internal migration.

In addition, there is a penchant for some who think about such matters to link any observed micropolitical change to epic events or moments of personal fortune or trauma. Societal events are assumed to get quickly translated into politics. Wars, recessions, scandals, depression, or personal misfortunes like losing a job or getting mugged are assumed to trigger a common, catholic, collective experience in those with similar fates. Those affected are assumed to seek retribution with the ballot as a direct result of their own self-interest.[3]

But if political environmental change fails to measure the effect of internal migration, or if macropolitical events or salient personal experiences are the reasons that the change monitored occurred, no systematic effects should have been observed among migrants. The quasi-experimental design would be flawed, the statistical methods inappropriate, and all of the preceding analysis dead wrong. Such null and random effects, however, are not observed. The statistical relationship between local political environmental change and micropolitical attributes of migrants exists.

The process of adjustment does not occur in the same fashion for everyone. The next chapter investigates some factors which can mitigate or accentuate the impact of internal migration.

Summary

1. Both congressional and presidential votes are influenced by the political environmental change a migrant experiences. The current political environment dominates previous environments in influencing the voting behavior of migrants. This persists even when disturbing socioeconomic effects are considered.
2. Incongruent migrants' political behavior shows the effect of their having lived in two areas dominated by different political parties. While the effects of the current local political environment dominate, the influence of the previous place of residence is also apparent for incongruent migrants.
3. Congruent migrants exhibit the most partisan voting behavior. They tend to be ardent party supporters.
4. Migrants' party identification is also influenced by the partisan congruence of their migration. Congruent migrants develop strong attachments to party. Incongruent migrants move toward partisan independence. Both traits are present even when individual-level partisanship is adjusted for socioeconomic, demographic, and age factors.
5. The level of commitment to politics as measured by the strength of party identification and turnout is diminished by a change of political environment.

Chapter 6

Resisting Political Environments

Give me a child until he is four years old and
I will give you a Catholic for life.

—Attributed to an Irish priest

Not every migrant adapts. This chapter investigates how family socialization experiences, political information, and age at time of migration act to minimize or accelerate adaptation to a new political
environment.

Adaptation has two sides. One suggests the image of a person
who is sensitive and smart and able to pick up the norms and behaviors of others. In new circumstances such as a new political environment, such a person can learn what is or what is not appropriate
behavior, and if he or she chooses, act accordingly. Another meaning
of adaptation carries the implication that an adaptable person is susceptible to peer pressure and especially the persuasive force of new
acquaintances. Intermixed with these opposing notions of adaptation are the early experiences a child may have had in the family, the
age a person is when changed environments are encountered, and
the sophistication and information possessed by the individual un-
dergoing change.

Early Political Socialization

Early socialization experiences are linked to an adult's ability to conform after experiencing a meaningful change of environment or to resist the pressures of change. From the very beginning, studies of political socialization showed that for the child, partisanship rapidly developed throughout grade school until around the age of eleven years and slowed down through adolescence and young adulthood (Easton and Dennis 1969; Hess and Torney 1967; Dawson, Prewitt, and Dawson 1977). Observations also showed that the level of partisanship in the child and adult samples were nearly the same (Hyman 1959:46; Greenstein 1965:74). The child's attitudinal development was viewed as being dependent on the parents' actions as was physical development. This dependency made resistance to parents difficult and therefore unlikely (Davies 1963).

Much like support for a specific religious sect, the party support and the strength of this attachment appeared mainly to stem from the family. The process of parental influence of a child's partisanship can be either direct, indirect, conflictual, or nonexistent. Some parents, raging partisans themselves, clearly indoctrinate their children with their particular persuasion. Alternatively, the political socialization process may work indirectly through the personal and social norms and values that are established in the home, still bringing about a clear set of political values. Parents who are personally efficacious and feel that their fate can be controlled, by example and instruction, may lead their children eventually to hold beliefs that society can be built and reformed if sufficient effort is involved. Whatever the process of transmission, the early political socialization literature pictured the child as a partisan reproduction of his or her parents. And why should this not be the case? When queried about their party attachment later on in life, in college or after, most who have a party loyalty have suggested that it stems from their parents.

The persistence of early partisan socialization appears to be born out by several findings that, once established in the child, the basic political orientations, such as partisanship, remain relatively constant throughout the life cycle. For example, the two NES panel studies of the adult population in the late 1950s and in the 1970s showed that a high degree of individual stability over time exists for party identification (Converse and Markus 1979). Thus the picture of partisan development seemed clear: once set in motion by the family, the individual persisted in his or her initial partisan orientation throughout life.

According to this view, then, a well-socialized migrant faced with a new partisan environment should be immunized from the social and political pressures to adapt. Indeed, as shown in Chapter 3, blacks from the rural South with weak or nonexistent partisanship became more involved in politics and more closely aligned with the Democratic party when they migrated to the urban, Democratic North. Few south-to-north black migrants prior to 1970 had parents who gave systematic partisan cues. Consequently their adaptation to the northern milieu was attributed to their lack of earlier socialized political experiences in the South.[1]

However, in the last decade, researchers have decreasingly emphasized preadult parental socialization as the sole determinant of political values. Jennings and Niemi have reported that the potential agreement between parents and their late adolescent children is considerably weaker than expected. The correlation between parents' party identification and that of their seventeen-year-old children is at the .5 level (*tau-b*) rather than at the .8 level (*tau-b*) when a respondent's partisanship is correlated with his or her recollection of parents' partisanship (Jennings and Niemi 1974:chaps. 2, 6).

Not only is the relationship between the parent and the late adolescent child not as strong as suspected, but also as the offspring moves into early adulthood, he or she often shifts categories of party identification. The partisan identification of younger adults seems clearly less stable over time than does that of older adults. When the 1965 sample of high school seniors was reinterviewed in 1973, their party identification was found to be less stable over time than that of the sampled adults (Jennings and Niemi 1981). The 1965–73 Youth-Parent Panel Study (YP) shows a level of stability of party identification over time similar to that reported in other adult panels of the 1950s and 1970s, around a .7 (*tau-b*). This is significantly higher than the .4 (*tau-b*) correlation found for the offspring. In terms of staying put within categories of party identification, only 58 percent of the young adults stayed within the same general party identification categories between 1965 and 1973, compared to over 70 percent of their parents.

It is likely that the original parent-child transmission is at minimum not the only mechanism by which partisan orientation is developed. Sears (1975) suggested several cogent reasons: (1) lack of consistency of parents' political attitudes; (2) low politicization level of the family; (3) variability in the affective ties with the family; (4) lack of simplicity and stability in the attitude object, the political party; and (5) competing agents of socialization that may either reinforce or combat the family's political norms. The first three points are tied to family dynamics. The last two rest on the existence of political forces external to the family, forces that may or may not reinforce family values

When the child is young, parents (the voting adults) must transmit clear, unambiguous partisan cues for attitudes to endure as a result of early socialization. But when the attitudinal independence from party among the adult population is high, relative to the past, and this independence takes the form of split-ticket voting or increased swing in the vote between the parties in important and highly visible elections, the ability of subsequent generations to pick up coherent partisan cues from the behavior of voting citizens must also be impaired. Thus, political cues from the family can vary substantially, being present or absent, clear or ambiguous. These distinctions matter, because children develop different partisan values as a function of the clarity of parental partisan cues. In families where the parents both identify with the same political party, the probability that the child will develop a similar attachment is approximately 1.5 times as great as when the cues are in conflict or not present (Brown 1977).

Measuring Family Partisan Background

This section presents the operational construct for the migrant's family partisan background. Any measurement of the family's partisan orientation must also consider both the direction of partisan influence in the family and the partisan congruence between the father and the mother or their surrogates.

The partisan composition of a family can range from homogeneous, when both parents are present in the home and also agree on important political values, to heterogeneous, when the parents are in conflict over political values, to nothing at all, when the parents are nonpartisan or absent. Operationally this occurs in several situations. A family background is coded Democratic or Republican when both parents are associated by the child as identifying with a single party, or when one parent supports a political party while the other is independent, apolitical, or absent, as is the case with single parent families. In these instances, a child is presumed to receive unambiguous partisan cues from the family or the politicized parent.

A family partisan background is coded split when the child is exposed to conflicting cues from the father and the mother. This situation occurs when each parent identifies with a different political party. Partisan cues coming from the split partisan family are assumed to be equally weighted between both parents.[2]

Finally, some children receive no partisan socialization from their families. To reflect this situation, families are coded nonpartisan when parents are perceived by their offspring as not having a party loyalty. A nonpartisan family background may result from both parents having no party identification. It can also stem from the children's not perceiving their parents as being interested in politics, voting in elections, or having a partisan identification.[3]

Political Environments versus the Family

As we have seen in the previous chapter, migration to incongruent political environments disrupts the individual's past partisan orientations and may reduce the persistence of early learned political values. The effect of migration to incongruent political environments is evident even among those families where the mother's and father's partisanships are in accord.[4] Among the high school seniors interviewed in 1965 and reinterviewed again eight years later, their own partisanship and the link with their parents' actual past partisanship show the strains of political environmental change brought on by migration. For congruent migrants, the cross-temporal correlation of their own party identification over the eight years is .37 (*tau-b*). The cross-temporal correlation drops to .29 (*tau-b*) for incongruent migrants. Stability is slightly higher for those living within or moving toward Republican contexts, and slightly lower for those in Democratic contexts.

When the comparison is made between a parent's actual partisanship as measured in 1965 and the young adult's partisanship as measured in 1973, congruent migrants have ties to a parent's past partisanship that are stronger (.40 *tau-b*) than are those of migrants changing partisan contexts (.27 *tau-b*).

The migrant's family political background is an important mitigating factor in determining a migrant's response to change in political environment. Migrants coming from solidly Democratic or Republican family backgrounds seem to respond differently from those whose families gave no clear partisan cues. As might be expected, young migrants from nonpartisan families appear to be affected the least by political environments. The data follow.

The average partisanship of migrants in the 1980 NES survey and the 1965–1973 YP panel study are illustrated in Figure 6.1 as a function of their perceived family partisan background and their current local political environment.[5]

The use of migrant data from both the 1965–1973 YP study and the

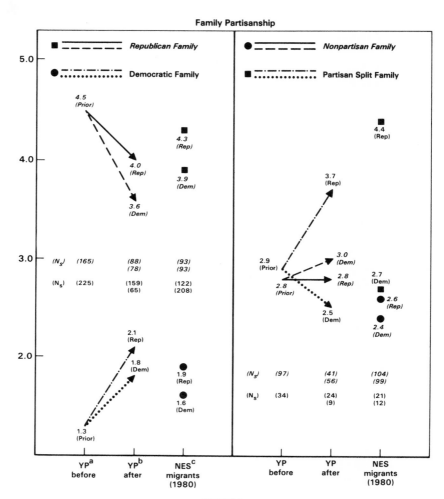

Figure 6.1

Mean Party Identification by Family Partisan Background and
Average Current Political Environment before and after Migration

Entries are average party identification scores, standard coding.

Sources: Youth-Parent Socialization Study, 1965, Center for Political
Studies, University of Michigan. Youth-Parent Panel, 1973, Center for
Political Studies, University of Michigan. American National Election
Study, 1980, Pre and Post Election Surveys, Center for Political Studies,
University of Michigan.

[a]Youth-Parent Socialization Study (1965).

[b]Youth-Parent Panel (1973).

[c]1980 NES.

1980 NES survey allows several perspectives to be examined simultaneously. The migrant's partisanship can be examined as a function of the partisan inclinations of his or her family both at a time when the individual is still at home and after migration when he or she is in a new political environment.

The average partisanship of the 521 sampled youths in their last year of high school prior to migration reflects their family's partisanship as expected. Those who were from pro-Democratic families heavily reflect the Democratic tendencies of their parents. Similarly, the high school partisanship of the 165 youths from pro-Republican families reflects that orientation. And 131 sampled youths from split partisan and nonpartisan families prior to migration edge toward partisan independence.

After migration the picture changes. Migrants from solidly Democratic families but living within a heavily Republican environment after moving still clearly think of themselves as Democratic partisans, but also show the influence of the new local Republican environment. Those from Democratic families who migrated to Democratic strongholds are predictably more Democratic than those in Republican areas.

Among migrants from Republican families, the same pattern can be seen. Those from Republican families who migrated to Democratic areas are within the range of self-identified Republicans, but less so then those who stayed within Republican areas.

A curious pattern can also be seen from the first panel of Figure 6.1. Migrants from politically homogeneous families, those where both parents have the same party identification, show in the years after migration a general shift in their party identification toward independence. Is this youthful rebellion against parents, a result of the tendency of the times to shift away from party, or a product of internal migration? Among youthful migrants, some will drift away from their families' political values during the years of early adulthood. This tendency may have increased during the period of the early 1970s, the years just before these migrants were reinterviewed. Tied in with abandoning parental values may be a move away from home. Considering the highly charged nature of the times in the late 1960s and early 1970s, effects of the uprooting stemming from changing political environments seem unremarkable. Among youthful migrants from homogeneous families, the patterns of partisanship still show the strong residue of the past plus the influence of present circumstance. A check on the response pattern with the 1980 NES data shows that migrants from self-reported homogeneous family backgrounds also have more or less the same partisanship given their current local political environment.

In addition, a comparison with nonmigrants in the YP study shows that it is migration, again, that plays a critical role in movement away from party. Nonmigrants show very little shift in partisan orientation from that found in their last year of high school, and indeed there is some evidence that they developed stronger identifications. Migration thus appears to have disrupted the development of party identification.

Migrants from families where the parents' loyalties to parties were split also show the clearest bent in the direction of the external political environment. While the number of observations is small, the evidence suggests that those from split families are susceptible to cues external to the family.

For migrants from nonpartisan families, migration to a Democratic or Republican political environment is not associated with the development of partisan identification. Migrants from nonpartisan families have scores very close to those of the political independent category, both before migration and after. Among migrants in the YP study whose families are nonpartisan, 65 percent consider themselves partisan independents. By contrast, well under half of the young adult migrants from homogeneous partisan or split partisan family backgrounds identified themselves as independents.

That the partisanship of migrants from nonpartisan families has no systematic relationship to a new political environment is counter to past research. Migrants with the weakest partisan family background were expected to be the most susceptible to the local political milieu. That they are not is something of a puzzle.

An individual has to receive information or perceive behavior from the political environment to be eventually influenced. In politics, voting, paying attention to and caring about the outcome of elections, discussing politics with others, and even trying to influence how others vote are forms of political involvement and commitment. Being committed to electoral politics is one way of becoming exposed to the forces of the political milieu. The reason that migrants from apolitical families remain more impervious than others to partisan forces after migration may be that earlier in life basic commitment to politics was not acquired.

Table 6.1 shows different aspects of political commitment by family background for migrants in 1973 and 1980. Across each category where the family provided some political cues, even if contradictory, migrants show a relatively high degree of commitment to and involvement with the political process. Yet among migrants who had apolitical parents, apathy and lack of interest in politics is not uncommon.

The lack of adaptation to the environment by migrants from apolitical families may be due to their low level of involvement in and commitment to politics. That their families failed to give them political resources made them unable to respond to political forces.

The average pull of local political environments on migrants, given in the originating family, holds even when demographic and social characteristics of the migrant are statistically controlled. The pattern of mean differences remains virtually unchanged when, as in the case of the 1980 migrants, the effects of the migrant's socioeconomic status, socioeconomic mobility, and age are removed in a linear fashion from the migrant's party identification. Again, the main effect determining party identification is still largely the family background, with a strong secondary influence of political environment.

In summary, the evidence from Figure 6.1 shows that early family political socialization does not fully immunize the migrant from new political environments. A uniform shift of the most politically socialized individuals occurs after migration. The movement of their party identification is away from their inherited partisanship and toward partisan independence. Migrants from nonpartisan family backgrounds seem the least influenced by political environments. This is contrary to previous research, which suggested that such migrants should be the most affected by new political environments. Migrants from split partisan families show the strongest response to the political environment entered after leaving the family.

Incongruent political migrations do not eliminate the strong influence of early childhood socialization. But again, even among those who are presumably politically socialized, migrants from politically homogeneous families, adjustment to a new political milieu is present even within a relatively short period of time. Thus what may be socialized in children along with specific partisan values is the need for identification and approval of others. This can lead to attitude adjustment and to political conformity later in life. But although early learned political values may not completely block the development of new political loyalties and beliefs, they can mitigate the effects of a new political environment. However, the mitigating force of a homogeneous family has to be understood in the cross-temporal dynamics of family political socialization. A child in the American family today where parents are both present is more likely than ever before to experience a split family political background. In 1970 only 18 percent of the children surveyed reported parents who disagreed in their partisanship, whereas by 1980 a third said they came from

Table 6.1. Levels of Political Commitment by Family Partisan Background for
Cross-Sectional and Young Adult Samples

| | Family Partisanship | | | | | | | |
| | Democratic | | Republican | | Split | | Nonpartisan | |
Sample Study:	NES[a]	YP[b]	NES	YP	NES	YP	NES	YP
% Having Partisan Identification	69	58	72	54	64	52	47	35
% Having High Psychological Involvement	25	51	26	55	25	38	19	44
% Voting in Last Election	74	72	79	82	58	82	59	58
% Persuading Others How to Vote	32	54	32	60	31	45	26	44

Source: Youth-Parent Panel Study, 1973, Center for Political Studies, University of Michigan. American National Election Study, 1980, Pre and Post Election Surveys, Center for Political Studies, University of Michigan.
[a]1980 NES.
[b]Youth-Parent Panel Study (1973).

politically split family backgrounds. These are the family background conditions, of course, that make it possible for environment to play a central role in determining party affiliation.

Political Knowledge

The commitment to prior political norms and beliefs, especially those nurtured by the family, may be most rigid among migrants with the greatest personal political resources. An indicator of political resources, of course, is factual political information and knowledge of the governing process. High levels of political information should represent a more detailed understanding of and experience with politics. A greater mass of political information should enable an individual to resist the forces of the external political environment.

High levels of political information and a sensitivity to political nuances may also translate into a greater capability of grasping and comprehending new partisan stimuli, a determinant to acceptance of new information. Those with a strong base of political information may be the most likely to understand and to act on the partisan information emitted by a new environment. The often subtle environmental cues may be missed by migrants less politically aware or lacking the minimal cognitive skills to understand a persuasive message. This issue was best outlined by McGuire (1969).

No survey question or scale completely picks up the information an individual uses to think politically. And most assuredly the mass survey instrument is a blunt tool for deciphering such cognitive capacities. Nonetheless, some facts should be common knowledge to a citizen well versed in politics, and familiar to anyone who even casually observes American politics.[6]

In Table 6.2, the evidence for the effect of political information is presented. Migrants have been divided into two political knowledge groups, those who are within the top quartile and those in the bottom of the political knowledge index. If the migrant's partisanship is compared across family and average partisan contextual experience, the impact of congruent or incongruent political cues may be understood better in light of the individual's political information base. Also included in Table 6.2 are the results of linear adjustment to remove the effects of socioeconomic and demographic factors.[7] For both raw and adjusted values, mean differences are computed across the average partisan context variable and reported at the bottom of the table. The greater the difference, the more likely that migrants have been influenced by their external partisan contexts. Nil or negative differences would mean that having lived in a given political environment did not have a separate effect on the migrant's party identification.

From both data sources and within categories of family partisan background, one generalization can be made: those with relatively low levels of political knowledge are less responsive to contexts encountered by migration than those with higher political information levels. Adjusting for socioeconomic factors only strengthens this finding. The socioeconomic attributes, which may induce different levels of political cognition, appear to leave the mean differences in partisanship unaffected for those with low levels of political information. The adjustment procedure only increases the differences for those with more political information.

Again, as was found in the earlier analysis, the presence of a homogeneous family political background makes the individual with a more extensive political information base more responsive to the external political environment. This holds whether the family of origin is Republican or Democratic.

Migrants from politically split families tend as before to respond to political context independent of family when both high and low lev-

Table 6.2. The Effects of Knowledge of Political Facts on Migrants' Partisanship Given Family Background and Average Partisan Context

Low Political Knowledge

| | | Family Partisanship | | | | | | |
| | | Democratic | | Republican | | Split | | Nonpartisan | |
Sample Study:		NES[a]	YP[b]	NES	YP	NES	YP	NES	YP
Average Partisan Context	Republican	2.3	2.2	3.4	4.3	3.2	5.1	2.4	3.2
	Democratic	2.1	1.8	3.4	3.8	2.8	3.3	2.3	3.1
Mean Difference		.2	.4	.0	.5	.4	1.8	.1	.1
Adjusted Mean Difference		.4	.2	.3	.3	nc[c]	nc	.7	.1
(N)		(169)	(75)	(73)	(47)	(18)	(12)	(64)	(32)

High Political Knowledge

| | | Democratic | | Republican | | Split | | Nonpartisan | |
Sample Study:		NES[a]	YP[b]	NES	YP	NES	YP	NES	YP
Average Partisan Context	Republican	2.5	2.1	4.0	3.5	4.0	3.0	2.3	2.7
	Democratic	1.8	1.3	3.4	3.2	2.6	2.1	2.5	2.7
Mean Difference		.7	.8	0.6	0.5	1.4	0.9	-.2	0
Adjusted Mean Difference		1.0	1.1	0.7	0.8	NA	NA	-.8	-.1
(N)		(88)	(64)	(57)	(58)	(12)	(11)	(20)	(27)

Source: Youth-Parent Panel Study, 1973, Center for Political Studies, University of Michigan. American National Election Study, 1970, Center for Political Studies, University of Michigan.
[a] 1970 NES.
[b] Youth-Parent Panel Study (1973).
[c] Not sufficient cases.

els of political knowledge are observed. Again, an insufficient number of cases made it impossible to adjust their partisanship for possible biasing effects.

Those migrants from apolitical family backgrounds, however, present something of a problem for what otherwise would be a simple generalization from the data at hand. The problem is that the two data sources show somewhat different outcomes. The raw, unadjusted mean estimates of partisanship show virtually no effect of external political environments irrespective of level of political information. When the adjusted estimates of migrants' average partisanship are turned to, this persists for those with high information levels and for migrants from the YP data. In the 1970 study, however, migrants from apolitical families and with low levels of political information have adjusted scores that reflect adjustment to political milieu. It is possible that political resources, or the lack of them, have a nonlinear relationship with adjustment to milieu. Those without any political resources, either inherited or acquired, adjust as do those with considerable political resources. On the other hand, those closer to a middle position having marginal political resources, a good education, high income, or relatively complete political information may know just enough to function in politics without the need to be sensitive to their surrounding milieus. Further research is needed to clarify this finding.

Environmental Adaptation and Age

Migrants may represent a segment of the population, especially at the time of entry into a new political environment, that is particularly sensitive to local partisan forces. To return to a point made earlier, at the time of migration many migrants may lack entrenched political values and consequently be open to persuasion by new experiences. In Chapter 2, I showed that individuals who have recently moved are considerably weaker in their commitment to politics than the stable population or than those migrants whose last move was some time ago. Across a variety of standard measures of political commitment, migrants at about the time they move appear to be potential partisans and available voters. Partly this is because migration is most likely to occur between eighteen and thirty-five years of age. Those who recently migrated are less committed to politics because they are younger than either nonmigrants or those who migrated at an earlier time. As a consequence, their experience with politics is not sufficient to thwart the pressures to adapt. This is an age-related hypothesis which predicts that a migrant's partisanship is more likely to conform to partisan environmental forces if migration occurs when young.

Figure 6.2 illustrates the proportion of migrants whose party identification is in agreement with their average partisan contextual experience. Migrants have been stratified both by their age at the time of their last migration and by the length of time they have lived in their current community. The latter split isolates age-related effects from those factors of assimilation that stem from prolonged exposure to the current milieu. Nil or slender differences between age groups would make a hypothesis about the importance of age at the time of migration less tenable. No differences between levels of exposure to the political environments would suggest that age effects dominate the previous findings and that independent of age, adaptation does not occur.

From the evidence at hand, the party identification of those younger than thirty-five when migrating is visibly more in accord with experienced partisan contextual forces. Irrespective of the length of time lived in the community, younger migrants adjust to their overall partisan environment at a faster rate and to a greater degree than older migrants.

The greater sensitivity of the young to their immediate political climate, however, is only part of the explanation. What is also evident from Figure 6.2 is that those over thirty-five at the time of their last migration also show the effect of contextual change, especially when exposed to the current partisan context for a prolonged period of time.

When migration occurs early in life, the adjustment to the political norms of the new setting should not involve much conversion of prior political attributes. When migration occurs later in life, however, subsequent adjustment raises at least the possibility that long-held political attributes will be challenged by exposure to new and different political forces. It is ironic, but adjustment among older groups, who are the least susceptible to the forces of partisan context, may result from the most severe form of individual change, conversion. As a consequence, the lower level of adjustment after migration for older migrants may reflect the greater difficulty of converting as opposed to mobilizing an individual.

Conclusion

During the period of late adolescence and early adulthood, the individual leaves home and often the nurturing environment of the

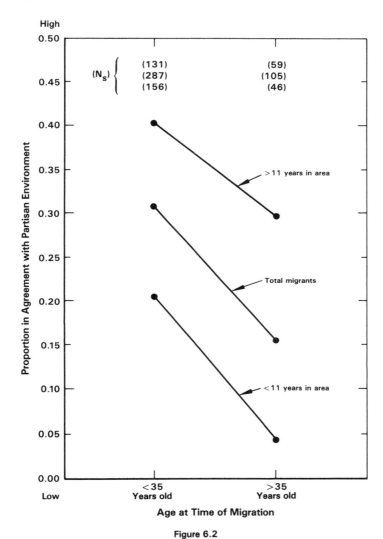

Figure 6.2

Agreement between Migrants' Party Identification and Overall Experience of Local Political Environments by Age at Time of Migration and Number of Years in the Current Environment

Source: American National Election Study, 1970, Center for Political Studies, University of Michigan.

home community as well. While the increasing efficiency of communication and transportation networks increases the likelihood that there will be some continuing support and information exchanged with the family, the break of proximal contact at least opens the individual to the outside world without the constant interaction with family and former friends. When this is coupled with the inherent vulnerability of those who are experiencing other life-cycle changes associated with moving into adulthood, normal resistance to the milieu could be weakened.

While social support may be needed by the migrant when confronting a new environment, it does not appear to be essential. Reference groups need not necessarily be proximate for their influence to be felt. Those moving into new settings may very well strongly identify with those they left at home, other groups sharing their political outlook, or even previous migrants to the new area. The possible effects of friends and peers can confound the more global effect of partisan context.

When external partisan environmental change was allowed to operate on the migrant's party identification within categories of family partisan background, it became obvious that the main factor determining the migrant's party attachment was still the family. Within the clearly homogeneous categories of perceived familial influence, migrants largely reflect the partisanship of their parents. However, even among these migrants, the partisan environment clearly had an influence in swaying the average identification in the direction of the environment.

What proved to be the most interesting was that those from apolitical families remained largely impervious to the contextual forces. Migrants from split partisan family backgrounds, however, adapted. A prime ingredient appeared to be a degree of commitment to and knowledge of politics, an attribute lacking in migrants with no family political background. Those with the highest levels of political information adapted the most to their average partisan context.

It is during the early adult years that the individual begins to become aware of the political world. Prior to that time the family by and large dominates the political life of the individual. Moreover, even if incongruent political information reaches the individual, the general level of interest in politics is usually so low that it probably has little impact. It is, then, during the early adult years that the individual begins to become aware of the political and, being freed from the exclusive dominance of family, is potentially susceptible to the forces of the outside environment.

Strong evidence suggests that partisan context influences the political attitudes and behavior of individuals. When internal migration reinforces a partisan environment, the micro effects of migration per se are of little lasting consequence. Environmental continuity allows for an uninterrupted development of partisan attributes. But when migration places the person in a different environment, the full development of partisanship—as revealed by both the congressional vote and party identification—is seriously attenuated.

Geographical mobility emerges as a significant event in the political socialization of an individual's life. The most typical migrants, the young, appear the most affected by their overall exposure to the external partisan environment, although older migrants with a greater period of exposure to the current milieu show similar effects as well.

Summary

1. Migration and the contextual change encountered through geographical mobility are significant to the continuing socialization of citizens. As to the partisanship of the family of origin, an individual's own partisanship reflects the early family experience even after migration to a different political environment.
2. But the susceptibility to new political environments is not thwarted by early socialization. On the contrary, those from homogeneous partisan families show clear evidence of the effect of living in a different partisan environment. Their own loyalty to the party of their families is weaker.
3. Individuals from apolitical families show no sensitivity to their external political environment. Their imperviousness seems to be a direct function of their lower level of political involvement.
4. Citizens with higher levels of political information are more likely to adapt to their immediate political environment than those with lower levels of information about politics and government.
5. The younger the migrant, the greater the likelihood that eventual partisanship will reflect the overall partisan contextual experience. Of secondary importance, but still significant, is the length of exposure to environment.

Part III

Adaptive Evolution

Chapter 7

Individualized Politics

'And now I'm in the world alone,
   Upon the wide, wide sea;
But why should I for others groan,
   When none will sigh for me?

—Byron, *Childe Harold's Pilgrimage*

The probability that a migrant will move from one political party to another is tied to contact with a different political environment. Migrant voters adapt their congressional and presidential votes fully to the pull of an incongruent local political environment. Psychological partisan loyalties, however, make way for political independence when local political environments are crossed. Movement to a new political party is supposed to be mitigated if the migrant is immune to new political information. Unfortunately the neat transfer of contagion theories concerned with the spread of diseases is not completely applicable to the social sciences. As the last chapter shows, those who should be the most immune to the consequences of changing political environments, the well socialized and the politically knowledgeable, are still likely to be influenced by their political environments.

Citizens who cross political environments, incongruent migrants, may be in the midst of change. As this chapter shows, an outcome of internal migration is to make citizens more sensitive to the political implications of their immediate personal experiences. Citizens voting in congressional and presidential elections rely more on their own economic self-interest than has been found in previous analysis. The political belief systems of migrants are also ordered and patterned in a fashion not traditionally accepted as a structured policy orientation. While congruent migrants tend to show relatively tightly woven, consistent belief systems, incongruent migrants tend to order policy attitudes on major issues of the day idiosyncratically, in an individualized style. The combination of votes linked to objective self-interest and idiosyncratic belief systems suggests that migrants' political actions and ideological beliefs do not fit the classic definition common in voting behavior. Rather, incongruent migrants exhibit tendencies of political decision making rooted in their own experiences rather than in a group orientation.

Attenuated Partisanship

The decline of political parties is illustrated by the secular drop in people's identification with parties (Wattenberg 1984). The meaning of this decline is best understood in the context of theory. When citizens lack a knowledge of what their own social values mean politically, when they are not aware of the policy implications of the electoral choices before them or the likely consequences of one outcome over another, in short, if they lack the cognitive skills needed for voting, the affective bond of a party attachment is believed to provide them with necessary cues to make reasonable political decisions.

It works in the following way. A political party is like a reference group. It translates for its members nonpolitical events and experiences into political reality. Partisanship works through latent group interest or overlaps with an identification with a social group. Like followers of a given religion who do not need to be theologians to follow the moral, religious precepts of their church, voters can arrive at reasonable decisions by knowing what their social group leaders think is good for people like them. Partisanship thus is a handle people use to think and act in politics. Not only can it help citizens vote in a way reasonably consistent with their group interests, it also informs them of their policy positions and which candidates they prefer (Campbell et al. 1960). The upshot is that party acts as a group symbol of what the individual is politically, as an extension of the ego into the political world.

A by-product of the symbolic nature of political party is that ordinary events in people's lives, or even major occurrences that affect everyone, get coded in symbolic ways to reflect the individual's partisanship rather than to mirror objective or even perceived personal self-interest. Consequently it is rare that personal experiences have a direct or an indirect effect on the vote (Sears et al. 1980).

But in the last two decades there has been a ratchetlike decline in the proportion supporting political parties. Consider a few examples. In 1952, 76 percent of those in labor unions identified with a political party, but only 62 percent of this group did so by the late 1970s. Similarly, in the early 1950s, the South averaged 79 percent identifying with a political party, but even with the rise of black mobilization and the rebirth of the Republican party in the South, only 64 percent expressed similar partisan loyalties in the late 1970s. Almost every demographic or social structural group exhibits similar tendencies.

The decline of political parties can be seen in two ways: by a decrease in the proportion psychologically identifying with parties, and by a weakening of the influence of party identification on the vote. In the 1950s, it was expected that approximately 6 percent of strong Democrats would defect in presidential contests; in the 1970s the figure increased to 14 percent. Among strong Republicans in the 1950s, 3 percent normally defected to the Democrats; in the 1970s it was 8 percent (Converse 1966; Miller 1979). Without political parties, what is to stop voters from relying more upon their own experiences when making electoral choices? And how is this related to internal migration?

Self-Interest and Migration

Of all groups, why should migrants be prone to political action based on their own self-interest? There seem to be several reasons. Migration often means that a person's group support is weakened by being outside of previous social networks. And as we saw in Chapter 5, when their political environment changes, migrants do support previous groups less. Migration also occurs when the individual is young. This symbolic predisposition, in this case partisanship, has not had a chance to take root. And finally, migrants are relatively vulnerable to outside pressures to conform, to be accepted in a new place. After migration, there are pressures to adapt to the existing norms of behavior and to be approved of by new co-workers, neighbors, and acquaintances. The solution to such social pressure is to behave politically in a fashion consistent with the new political environment. Migrants conform to this expectation.

At the same time, migrants neither stay the way they were prior to migration nor convert to match those in their new environment. They are citizens who do not fit easily into the existing pattern of partisan categories, and as such they may have to rely on their own wits to make political decisions. And somewhat paradoxically, symbolic predispositions presume a shared, even collective commitment on the basis of how people believe they are commonly affected by a problem. While migrants behave like everyone else, they do not think like everyone else or have similar attitudes—especially toward parties. Something else besides partisan values is pressuring their vote to match up with the political environment.

Finding Elusive Self-Interest

The analysis of the connection between personal self-interest and politics to date has mostly focused on economic self-interest, especially as it relates to income, family finances, unemployment, and concerns about the rate of inflation. Aggregate, time series analysis has provided the only strong support of the direct influence of macroeconomic variables on the vote (Kramer 1971; Bloom and Price 1975).

Yet when the same political questions concerning the impact of personal economic situation, or even noneconomic personal experiences based on health status, crime, or local school busing are tested with micro data, no direct effects are found (Sears et al. 1980). Symbolic factors completely dominate the explanation of most micropolitical phenomena. Effects that are reported have to date been only very indirect, influencing individual attitudes that eventually influence behavior. Fiorina, for example, has shown that personal economic factors are related to general evaluations of macroeconomic performance and that both in turn influence the citizen's evaluation of presidential performance and eventually even influence partisan identification (Fiorina 1981:chap. 9). The vote is not directly influenced by personal economic situation.

But even the meager support for the micropolitical relation between expressed personal economic situation and economic policy performance has been called into question because of serious methodological and theoretical problems. One set of criticisms concerns the survey format within which questions are asked of respondents. The second concerns the logic of using sample surveys to detect personal self-interest.

Sears and Lau (1983) have shown with a clever experiment that relationships between personal economic conditions, like the respondent's family's financial situation, and major political preferences may be inflated if the self-interest items are asked either right before or after political items. They suggest that political items may be personalized if they are asked soon after questions concerning the respondent's economic situation. Or subjective questions about economic condition can be politicized if asked after those concerning important political preferences. The problem is solved by keeping the two sets of questions far apart in the survey instrument.

Even when question order is correct, the discrepancy persists between aggregate, time series findings showing a relationship between macroeconomic conditions and national election outcomes on the one hand and research based on mass surveys which does not show a relationship between economic self-interest and voting behavior on the other. Jacobson and Kernell (1981:12) suggest that the gap may be the result of a political singularity: a small segment of the public, because of their economic situation, attach themselves psychologically to the political party of the candidate they plan to support. And if both partisan loyalty and the vote move together as a result of personal or national economic forces, this would only be found in a longitudinal analysis and not within a single survey. This is very similar to a suggestion made by Kramer (1983), which is that national cross-sectional survey data used for investigating the effect of personal economic fluctuations is simply not appropriate. He argues that the responses to cross-sectional surveys may be the product of both government-induced factors or exogenous considerations particular to the individual respondent—factors that are not necessarily political. Hence, a survey would fail to find meaningful relationships between self-interest items and the vote. Kramer also suggests that both incumbency effects and the business cycle itself could bias the relationship between a personal economic situation and the vote, inducing strong relations in some years or null or even negative ones in other years. However, within the period from 1960 to 1980, Kramer's concern does not appear to be a serious problem (Kiewiet 1983:49).

Defining self-interest based rational action is theoretically just as problematic as proving its existence. Traditional utility theory has suggested that a rational person is one who maximizes expected utility. That is, a rational actor is one who can "assign a utility to consequences, estimate the likelihood that each consequence will be obtained, calculate the utility of an act and choose an act of maximum utility" (Burk 1977:247). This definition can, however, lead to a few problems: the sure thing paradox and its generalized companion, the variance paradox (Allais 1953). And even when the estimation of object utility is relaxed and a subjective expected utility is used, the calculated utility can still be tautological: any action can be assumed to maximize expected utility; otherwise it would not be done (Rapoport 1966).

When objective or subjective self-interest is not the ultimate criterion, rationality may be operationally defined as consistent and complete preferences at any given point in time (Stroltz 1955:165–80). And presumably irrationality, or at least nonrationality, is found when political attitudes or actions are inconsistent. This is close to accepted indications of randomness. The difference, of course, is that the individual's reasons and responses to a personal stimulus for change may make a change from past action rational even if a pattern or degree of external consistency is not evident. But the reasons given are often linked to objective or perceived self-interest. Needless to say, the different implications of the meaning of rational self-interest create an opportunity for real confusion.

Examining nonpolitical experiences, such as aging and life-cycle change, social mobility and geographical mobility, that affect the individual's economic situation (and hence the individual's self-interest) and specifying exactly what gives these exogenous factors political importance can reveal those otherwise unobservable experiences and their hidden political consequences. This analysis, of course, focuses on the embedded political consequences of population movement.

Votes and Personal Economic Self-Interest

Table 7.1 shows the summary estimates of how well the actual vote is predicted by economic self-interest variables with and without symbolic measures of partisanship and ideology. The economic self-interest component is composed of one or several objective experiences of either the respondent or the head of the household— whether he or she is currently unemployed, has experienced unemployment during the last twelve months, is working but under adverse financial conditions such as reduced hours or too many hours (which might occur with a second job), or is in a position below his or her qualifications. Self-interest is also measured by subjective appraisals of the respondent's family's current and past economic situation. And because inflation and unemployment were important considerations in 1980, the respondent was asked whether inflation has hurt the family, whether the family's income has kept pace with rising prices, and whether a major wage earner in the household was in fear of losing his or her job.

The approach taken is to show the summary fit both of simple

Table 7.1. Summary of Congressional and Presidential Votes as a Function of Symbolic and Economic Self-Interest Variables in 1980

| | Estimated Model | | | |
| | Symbolic[a] plus Self-Interest[b] | | Self-Interest | |
	PV[c]	CV[d]	PV	CV
Total Migrants	.456**	.241*	.053	.019
Contextual Change				
Congruent	.496**	.204*	.068	.049
Incongruent	.608**	.427**	.256*	.120*

Source: American National Election Study, 1980, Pre and Post Election Surveys, Center for Political Studies, University of Michigan.

Entries are R^2.

** p less than .0001

* p less than .001

[a]Symbolic variables: party identification and liberal-conservative ideological orientation.

[b]Self-Interest variables: unemployment, unemployed in the last twelve months, reduced hours, too many hours, present position below qualifications, fear of being unemployed, inflation hurt family, income not keeping up with inflation, family financial condition worse last year, family financial condition expected to be worse next year.

[c]PV: Presidential vote for Reagan or Carter.

[d]CV: Congressional vote Democrat or Republican.

additive models for equations that include symbolic political variables and of those that have only personal self-interest variables. Separate equations were estimated both for the congressional and presidential votes for the total set of migrants and for the two central analysis groups, congruent and incongruent migrants.

In Table 7.1, for all migrants considered at once, the effect of dropping the symbolic variables, especially party identification, and examining just the effects of self-interest is obvious. Self-interest variables contribute nothing significant to the overall explanation of either vote preference. Roughly 5 percent of the presidential vote and 2 percent of the variance in the congressional vote are explained by pure self-interest. This is not surprising and fits in well with previously published results. For congruent migrants, reported in the second row of Table 7.1, the same occurs when the vote is examined as a function of self-interest. The voting preferences of these migrants are a product of factors other than objective self-interest. Not too surprisingly, congruent migrants, who showed high levels of developed partisanship in previous analyses, rely upon their party identification as the most important determinant of either vote decision.

The votes of incongruent migrants respond differently to economic self-interest. In the full model with both the symbolic measures of partisanship and ideology and the economic self-interest items, the overall explanatory power of the model is considerably greater than for the total set of migrants or congruent migrants. Close to 61 percent of the variability in the presidential vote and 43 percent of the congressional vote are explained. The difference appears to lie in the greater influence that several measures of personal economic self-interest have on the vote decisions. When only the economic self-interest component is used to estimate presidential and congressional votes, around 26 percent and 12 percent, respectively, of the variance in the vote decision are accounted for. That these equations are significant is even more surprising given the relatively small number of cases underlying the estimation models.

Chapter 5 examined the degree to which migrants adjust their votes to match the current political environment. It revealed that political behavior more readily matched the political forces in the new environment than was previously assumed even among incongruent migrants. And it is certainly true that incongruent migrants adjust their vote far more than their party identification. Left to speculation was the reason for the behavioral adjustment that occurred.

In Table 7.2 the vote is examined in a slightly different way. The dependent variable, voting in accord with the environment, is simply whether the migrant's vote agrees with dominant partisan tendencies of the current political environment. What is estimated by the equations is the likelihood that voting in accord with the environment is a product of symbolic orientations or is rooted in the migrant's personal self-interest. And as with the models predicting the actual vote, the effects of both the symbolic plus self-interest components and the self-interest factor alone are shown.

While the explanatory level is generally lower than in the previous table, the same pattern can be found. Incongruent migrants tend to show that their votes in accord with the current political environment are clearly influenced by their economic situation. Of the variables specified, the most important considerations in determining the agreement between the congressional vote and the environment are having had a family wage earner experience unemployment during the last 12 months and believing that the present job is below the level for which the respondent or the head of household is qualified. For presidential voting, agreement with the current environment is related strongly to present unemployment in the family, the fear of unemployment, and having the hours of a major wage earner cut back.

These analyses show that migrants end up relying on objective

Table 7.2. Summary of Congressional and Presidential Votes in Accord with the Current Partisan Environment as a Function of Symbolic and Self-Interest Variables

	Estimated Model			
	Symbolic[a] plus Self-Interest		Self-Interest	
	PV_e	CV_e	PV_e	CV_e
Total Migrants	.053	.059	.003	.004
Contextual Change				
Congruent	.140*	.148*	.108	.127
Incongruent	.258**	.342**	.195*	.211*

Source: American National Election Study, 1980, Pre and Post Election Surveys, Center for Political Studies, University of Michigan.
Entries are R^2.
** p less than .001
* p less than .01
[a] See Table 7.1 for heading definitions.

self-interest. For both their voting adaptation to current political environment and their straight voting calculations, incongruent migrants appear to show significant use of their objective and subjective personal experiences. While it cannot be stated for sure, I think it likely that they behave this way because of their diminished partisanship. Incongruent migrants are more likely to base their prime political decisions on those situations closest to them and their families. Migrants may fill the gap left by what would have been their partisan loyalty by increasingly relying on their own personal experiences.

In experimenting with the electoral role of personal economic situation for migrants, I find a curious consistency which cannot be statistically removed. Party identification is significant in all the estimated models and is by far the single most important variable in the vote decision. But separately moving party identification in and out of the model did not produce the same effect on the various self-interest measures as did the separate insertion or exclusion of liberal-conservative self-placement. Ideology seems to have a curious interacting effect with self-interest, even though, when directly tested, such interaction components strain statistical inference. At the end of this chapter some analysis is presented to interpret this finding.

I do not think it surprising that migrants show traits of self-interest that have not been found in a general canvasing of a cross-sectional public. Migrants may be more motivated to seek economic rewards and benefits. They have experienced greater costs and consequently may have greater expectations about future economic pay-offs from migration. But aside from weaker partisanship, incongruent migrants may end up thinking differently about politics. If they are prone to adapt to their new setting, they also tend to know more about politics and to have more experience with politics, starting with their families. But do they think differently as a result of migrating across political environments? The next section takes up the question of the cognitive aspects of contextual change.

Personal Political Beliefs

Individualized thinking in politics can be manifested through the political attitudes of migrants, especially in the formation of their policy beliefs on major issues of the day. A great deal is known about the theoretical aspect of the formation and maintenance of policy attitudes. Two key concepts are consistency and stability.

The ideological consistency in the linkage among policy preferences and the constancy of those preferences over time involve traits of sophisticated and informed political thinking (Converse 1964). Issue consistency is often measured as the degree of aggregate similarity from one issue to the next. The idea is that since issues of public policy are often in ideological bundles, the citizen whose policy preferences are dictated by more general ideological values should integrate and respond to specific issues on the basis of general beliefs. Thus a person holding liberal racial attitudes should be in favor of a wide variety of civil rights policies. A person abhorring the government's role in the economic affairs of citizens should express this across a wide variety of social welfare issues. The more such values influence an individual, the more differentiated political thinking is. When belief systems are both integrated and differentiated, they are also assumed to be more complex (Bennett 1975:chap. 3). When political belief systems are more complex, they tend both to be associated with greater amounts of political information and to be more stable (Converse 1964). Individuals with complex belief systems are also assumed to be more tolerant of ambiguity and heterodoxy because they are better able to withstand the personal stress of change as a result of their ability to hold conflicting ideas in a more abstract and theoretical fashion (Lane 1983). By contrast, those without consistent and stable belief systems are less able to withstand the short-term pressures from the external environment to change and, as a consequence, show less consistent and less stable policy preferences. It is assumed that such citizens' policy preferences are neither the product of ideology nor in-depth normative opinions about the relationship between state and man.

Discounted as a possibility that may be between the extremes of complex versus simple belief systems is that individuals hold personal, idiosyncratic policy preferences. Such belief systems would be based on positions on policy questions that have an implicit logic to the individual but that vary considerably from one person to the next. Idiosyncratic belief systems would not necessarily be consistent in the aggregate.

If individual preferences for a given policy outcome do not relate to other policy preferences, they will not form neat aggregate patterns. However, if single issue preferences are based on personal beliefs systems, they should be relatively stable over time (Converse 1964). This pin in the argument has never been supported. In fact, most of the evidence suggests that those who have unstructured belief systems tend to have unstable beliefs as well. Further, the presence of idiosyncratic belief systems was not seriously investigated because the concept was never needed. Citizens were tied to political parties that gave them a solid base for understanding electoral politics. And when the typical voter's lack of political information and marginal interest and involvement in elections was factored in, the likelihood that he or she would construct a personal view of politics was remote.

When partisan values were more widespread, they provided powerful and long-term attitudinal predispositions for an individual's response to issues of the day. Indeed for some issues, it is likely that the stronger the partisan orientation, the more likely the individual embodied the ideological tendency associated with the political party. While it is a common view that the weakening of party ties in the mass public is associated with a rise in greater ideological thinking (Verba, Nie, and Petrocik 1979), it may be that the absence or reduction of partisanship actually undercuts what structuring of policy orientations does exist on the basis of issues underlying a partisan alignment.

However, once individuals are not bound by the bonds of group attachment and if they have the skills to do so, they may fashion positions on issues and between issues according to personal considerations. If this is true, of course, it would suggest the possibility that migration may play an even more complex role in the development of citizens' political attitudes. Let us turn to some data.

From the 1980 NES data, among the twenty issues of policy concern about which respondents were asked, three dimensions define the most central policy themes: social liberalism, economic welfare, and traditionalism.[1] The first two policy domains represent the types of issues that have dominated the partisan differences between Democrats and Republicans during the last fifty years. The social liberalism dimension plays concerns about race-related issues against those about military and defense-related priorities. The second dimension, economic welfare, monitors public perception about macroeconomic problems, the power of the federal government as well as the government's role and responsibilities in providing for social welfare. The third dimension, traditionalism, is not a set of issues which have historically separated the major political parties. They are, however, issues that refer to the traditional role of women in society and the role of prayer in public schools. This type of issue concerns, at least in the late 1970s and early 1980s, has not defined political parties and their candidates as clearly as have national economic issues. Hence on issues concerning women, abortion, and school prayer, party loyalty or even a traditional ideological viewpoint do not easily guide a citizen's preference.

The interitem correlation of single policy issues within each of these policy dimensions can be used as a measure of attitude consistency. High interitem correlations within policy domain would indicate a reasonable degree of aggregated consistency; low correlations would suggest the opposite.

From the evidence presented in Table 7.3, it is clear that the type of local political environmental change migrants have experienced is related to their developed belief systems. Across the first and second dimensions, among those with environmentally congruent migration experiences, the aggregate level of consistency is high in an absolute sense, and considerably greater than for those who changed political environments when migrating. In the first dimension, social liberalism, the average interitem correlation for congruent migrants is over .7, whereas for incongruent migrants it is around .3. A similar pattern is found between the two migrant groups for the second dimension, economic welfare.

Again, as has been shown earlier and stressed several times, congruent migrants end up with stronger partisan identifications than incongruent migrants. For issues such as those that define the social liberalism and economic welfare policy domains, the stronger partisan attachments of congruent migrants appear to have the effect of inducing a more cohesive and structured set of policy orientations. Across issues that do not have a clear set of partisan cues developed in conjunction with the given policy alternatives, such as those found in the traditionalism scale, the differences between the two migrant groups collapse. Incongruent migrants, who as a group

Table 7.3. Attitude Consistency within 1980[a] Policy Domain by Contextual Congruency of Migration

	Social Liberalism[a]	Economic Welfare[b]	Traditionalism[c]
Contextual Change			
Incongruent	.32[d]	.27	$\boxed{.24}$
Congruent	$\boxed{.76}$	$\boxed{.48}$	.22

Source: American National Election Study, 1980, Pre and Post Election Surveys, Center for Political Studies, University of Michigan.

[a]*Social Liberalism*: Defense spending, aid to minorities, speed of civil rights movement, school busing.

[b]*Economic Welfare*: Liberal-conservative position, government services, inflation-unemployment trade-off, standard of living, government too powerful.

[c]*Traditionalism*: Women equal, equal rights amendment, prayer in school.

[d]Weighted average inter-item Pearson correlation within policy domain.

have weaker levels of partisanship, tend to have the same degree of attitude consistency as do congruent migrants.

As to the aggregate stability of policy attitudes, there appears to be a difference, again based on contextual change. But in this case, incongruent migrants have higher levels of attitude stability for issues of public policy than are found for congruent migrants.[2]

Table 7.4 presents the aggregate attitude stability levels for repeated policy issues and liberal-conservative self-placement. Each cell entry is the average correlation over the three waves of the 1980 NES panel. For each repeated policy item, the level of attitude stability is higher for migrants with incongruent experiences associated with movement than for those with congruent experiences. While the magnitude of the differences between the two migrant groups is not great, the differences are consistent across each issue asked in the panel.

Stability is most commonly shown by the level of correlation between items over time. Correlation analysis, which measures the differences between two populations, depends upon the populations being equally heterogeneous in their attitudes. What is obvious from the earlier analysis is that migrants differ in terms of their voting behavior and partisan identification depending upon their overall political environmental experience. The shift in the political composition of these two types of migrants may ultimately underestimate the level of attitude stability among incongruent migrants.

An individual-level measure of item stability circumvents the distribution problem of homogeneous populations and may give us a clearer understanding of the political effects of migration beyond partisanship.[3] The resulting measure can be thought of as the magni-

Table 7.4. Aggregate Attitude Stability by
Contextual Congruency of Migration

	Defense Spending	Soviet Détente	Government Services	Inflation-Unemployment Trade-Off	Liberal-Conservative
Contextual Change					
Incongruent	.59[a]	.49	.43	.38	.49
Congruent	.55	.44	.40	.34	.37

Source: American National Election Study, 1980, Panel Wave P1 through P3, Center for Political Studies, University of Michigan.
[a]Average, *tau–b* statistic, $(t_1 - t_2)$, $(t_2 - t_3)$, $(t_1 - t_3)$.

tude of the individual mean change in policy position over time. The smaller the value, the higher the attitude stability.

From Table 7.5, across the set of policy items in the 1980 panel, the change in response over time is lower for the total set of incongruent migrants than for that of the congruent migrants. For most of the items, in addition, the standard deviation of the average fluctuation for incongruent migrants is in a lower range than for congruent migrants.

When the length of time in the community is considered with the level of individual stability on policy differences, the influence of partisan contextual experience is increased. With few exceptions, congruent migrants who have lived in their current community for more than eleven years show *higher* rates of change in their policy positions than are found among incongruent migrants. Incongruent migrants tend to solidify their policy positions over time.

The combined evidence of a diminished party attachment and greater dependency on self-interest along with the rise of a more idiosyncratic belief system suggests that incongruent migration may produce substantially different actors in electoral politics. Such migrants tend to be more individualistic and personal in calculating major political decisions.

One final point is noteworthy. Earlier, I suggested that the liberal-conservative orientation as a measure of ideology showed a curious connection to economic self-interest. From the evidence in Table 7.5, the measure that shows the greatest degree of stability is ideology. Among incongruent migrants, it is safe to suggest that ideology becomes over time about twice as stable as issue beliefs. Is it possible that ideological symbols are being ingested by citizens as they lose their partisan symbols?

One explanation may be that a form of ideology identification is replacing partisan identification. The 1964, 1972, and 1980 elections each injected a strong ideological component into the national politi-

Table 7.5. Individual Attitude Stability by Partisan Contextual Congruency of Migration

	Defense Spending		Government Services		Soviet Détente		Inflation-Unemployment Trade-Off		Liberal-Conservative	
	Total	>11 Years	Total	>11 Years	Total	>11 Years	Total	>11 Years	Total	>11 Years
Contextual Change:										
Incongruent	.397[a]	.420	.401	.402	.456	.407	.424	.418	.323	.256
	(.330)	(.400)	(.276)	(.274)	(.360)	(.396)	(.346)	(.343)	(.313)	(.231)
Congruent	.401	.493	.507	.601	.461	.551	.480	.585	.363	.409
	(.405)	(.542)	(.326)	(.402)	(.350)	(.430)	(.378)	(.416)	(.384)	(.327)

Source: American National Election Study, 1980, Panel Wave P1 through P3, Center for Political Studies, University of Michigan.
[a]The lower the coefficient, the *higher* the attitude stability.

cal environment (Nie et al. 1979; Miller and Shanks 1983). This occurred mostly through candidates and the positions they were perceived to have taken. Issue- and candidate-driven ideology may be
an *affective* response rather than a *cogitative* quality in the individual.

Affective ideology may rest upon the association of issue positions
or a particular candidate's issue positions with ideology. In this case
the issue couched in ideological rhetoric gives a fairly concrete meaning to the ideological term. This, of course, is exactly the opposite of
a cognitive-based ideology, where the ideology belief is used to
evaluate issues or candidates.

Affective ideology may be the product of the declining utility of
social groups as providers of cues for political behavior. Party as the
summation of past group political experience may be meaningless to
the nonaligned or nongroup-oriented citizen. And for those whose
supports for party have been removed, such as incongruent migrants, the world may not be viewed through partisan lenses, but
through an epigeal form of ideology. This form lacks the directive
qualities of a full-blown ideology, and may, like partisanship, work as
an ideology by proxy without the latent group component.

If ideology for migrants is an affective attribute, it is not likely to
mold personal experiences or external events into votes. Political ob-
jects such as issues or candidates or events of the day would need to
be precoded in terms of "liberalness" or "conservativeness" to be of
use to those with affective ideologies. Yet if the ideological predisposition of incongruent migrants is a cognitive attribute, it may serve
functionally as a political predisposition for migrants. In the case at
hand, with the differential ability of incongruent migrants to react to
their own personal experiences, the meaning of their liberalness and
conservativeness deserves a closer look.

Individualism and Collective Responsibility

At an earlier time, individualism had a positive political tone,
even a moral caste to it. Individualists set out to restore political
power to people. They were antimachine and sought to provide for
popular rule through such political instruments as recall, initiative,
and referendum control over elected politicians. They called for citizens to vote independently from party (Hays 1957:92). And from the
candidates that individualists supported, there was a stream of pro-
posals to aid workers, especially women workers, and children and
to seek national, collective goals instead of those of labor and business. Of course, this was in the first decade of this century.

More recently, however, the notion of individual as rational actor has taken on a different meaning, one stripped of collective spirit. And there has been a long-standing sense, engendered by economic models of rationality, that a rational individual is politically selfish and not predisposed to seek collective, government-controlled solutions to perceived social or economic problems. As we have seen so far in this chapter, migrants hold several micropolitical traits which may lead them to also hold policy positions more oriented toward the individual. Does this extend into the policy arena as well?

Table 7.6 presents the policy orientations of migrants separated by their partisan contexts. Three issues—the reduction of government spending, aid to minorities, and the guarantee of a job and good standard of living—represent the type of social welfare propositions commonly associated with the conflict between individual initiative to gain social and economic rewards and the responsibility of government to somehow guarantee a level of quality of life. Two other issues, Soviet détente and defense spending, are presented because they represent foreign policy concerns that are also tied to underlying social values. And finally, the distribution of the respondent's own self-placement on the liberal-conservative dimension is shown. Again, if a type of migration experience, especially incongruent migration, is associated with the development of a different, more individualistic orientation, it may be visible from the perspective of these issues.

The policy traits of migrants seem clearly to be influenced by their current partisan context. For those who are living within or moving toward pro-Republican environments, there is a clear tendency to be more conservative on social welfare issues and in their own self-identification. Within the set of all those living in Republican-dominated environments, however, incongruent migrants seem to be the least conservative of the lot, reflecting perhaps their earlier exposure to the more liberal policies of the Democratic party. It is only on the issue of aid to minorities that incongruent migrants tend to be more likely than congruent Republican migrants to believe in the idea that individuals should get ahead on their own.

On the other hand, migrants living in pro-Democratic environments seem to reflect if not a liberal orientation, then a less conservative one. Both in terms of their own ideological self-identification and across each of the social welfare issues, migrants moving within or toward Democratic areas are more inclined to support the role of government in helping minorities and in guaranteeing a job and a standard of living. In addition, they are more likely to believe that government services should not be cut back by reducing spending. Again, incongruent migrants within Democratic areas tend to be as

Table 7.6. Relative Issue Position by Partisan Contextual Change

	Reduce Spending	Guarantee Standard of Living	Aid to Minorities	Soviet Détente	Defense Spending	Liberal-Conservative
Contextual Change						
Congruent Republican	+38[a]	+35	+24	+24	+52	+17
(N)	(52)	(42)	(42)	(42)	(52)	(53)
Mixed Republican	+19	+35	+44	-5	+71	+14
(N)	(48)	(40)	(41)	(41)	(48)	(48)
Incongruent Republican	-4	+24	+40	+20	+60	+21
(N)	(53)	(45)	(45)	(45)	(53)	(52)
Incongruent Democratic	-13	+1	+19	-8	+44	+1
(N)	(76)	(69)	(69)	(69)	(76)	(74)
Mixed Democratic	-19	+2	+30	-7	+65	+1
(N)	(43)	(43)	(43)	(43)	(43)	(42)
Congruent Democratic	-10	+7	+11	+4	+39	+14
(N)	(96)	(82)	(82)	(82)	(95)	(94)

Source: American National Election Study, 1980, Pre and Post Election Surveys, Center for Political Studies, University of Michigan.
[a]Categories of issue questions #1 to #3 are subtracted from #4 to #7. The larger the difference (PDI), the more conservative the average response.

liberal as congruent migrants on questions of government spending and the guarantee of jobs.

The effect of context on foreign policy is not as strong, but it is not negligible either. Those within Republican environments are more likely to be leery of the Soviets and in favor of boosting defense expenditures. Those within Democratic environments are more likely to believe that it is important to get along with the Soviets and are also in favor, but less strongly, of a defense buildup.

In general, across both domestic and foreign issues, there is no tendency for those who have crossed partisan contexts to withdraw their support for collective solutions any more than would be predicted on the basis of their current context. Again, as was observed in terms of both the voting behavior and party identification of incongruent migrants, they tend to reflect their previous partisan experiences in their current policy orientations. However, in the case of the selected policy and ideological orientations examined here, there seems to be a greater degree of adaptation to the current partisan area and separation from the previous one than was observed for partisan actions or votes.

Conclusion

In his classic criticism of the economic model of rationality, Plamenatz argued that "how men see themselves is intimately connected with their mental images of the community; they are not mere competitors however benevolent, in markets for the supply of personal wants; they are members of society, and their hopes and feelings both for themselves and others, would not be what they are apart from their group loyalties" (1958:175). What Plamenatz would probably say as well is that community is not a place where one lives but instead is a structure of loyalties to groups—occupational and professional, religious, ethnic, and even political. Personal links to similar people, he might say, have replaced personal links to community.

Yet migrants, especially those who may have their political loyalties weakened or stripped away completely by the forces of changing political environments, are likely to make political decisions and eventually adapt their most basic political beliefs and loyalties on the basis of their own personal experiences. The way they think about politics seems to be a construct of their own individuality. But it is also the case that among those migrants most susceptible to the pull of self-interest and idiosyncratic thinking, there does not appear to be a diminution in their collective conscience.

It may be that migrants who rely upon their own self-interest are doing so as a way of coping with the loss of group identity and supporting networks of an earlier time. While incongruent migrants may lack the fully developed partisan loyalty of nonmigrants or congruent migrants, they do not appear to be partisan renegades within their new communities. They vote with their communities and they appear to be pulled into the web of policy preferences common to people who reside in similar political milieus.

Summary

1. Both the congressional and presidential votes of incongruent migrants appear to have a significant economic self-interest component. Such relationships are not found for either the total set of migrants nor for congruent migrants.
2. Across three-issue policy dimensions, congruent migrants show a greater degree of aggregate attitude consistency than is found for incongruent migrants. This is especially true for issues related to social liberalism and economic welfare. The traditionalism dimension does not show a difference in the aggregate consistency between the two groups.
3. For measures of aggregate- and individual-level cross-temporal attitude stability, incongruent migrants are more likely to maintain stable political beliefs than are congruent migrants. This trait also seems to increase over time. The combined cognitive attributes of a low degree of attitude consistency and high levels of attitude stability in policy preferences are indicative of idiosyncratic belief systems.
4. Liberal-conservative orientation shows the highest level of attitude stability. It is possible that an affective ideological orientation may be forming among incongruent migrants.
5. Across a variety of social welfare and foreign policy areas, migrants appear to take on the ideological orientations of their partisan contexts. Those in Republican areas tend to become more conservative, those in Democratic contexts less conservative. Incongruent migrants tend to reflect their past partisan experiences across several policy dimensions. Incongruent migrants, in spite of evidence that they rely upon self-interest in making political judgments, do not appear to shun collective solutions to public policy problems.
6. The conclusion is that migrants who change contexts are in the midst of personal political change.

Chapter 8

Political Evolution

The *little* things that offend a sense of order are
the most disturbing.

Stephen Jay Gould, *Agassiz in the Galápagos*

The findings and implications of Chapters 1 through 7 are recapitu-
lated next. Following a summary of each chapter, I conclude the book
with a discussion of the role of geographical mobility in mass
politics.

Recapitulation

The first section of the book concerns theory and description. The
main controversy discussed, and the one which informs the analysis
throughout this book, stems from the tension between competing
theories of political socialization. One perspective argues that individuals faced with the conditions of change tend to persist in actions
and attitudes learned early. This perspective argues that the individual migrant who was politically socialized early in life should not
be influenced by changes of political environment encountered as an
adult. This view, of course, represents the accepted reason that migration was not thought to be a source of micropolitical change.

A second theoretical perspective argues that socialization is a continuous process because adults remain open to the effects of changed
circumstances. The "lifelong openness" model suggests that citizens
are sensitive to their own personal experiences and can therefore

translate those experiences into political behavior and political beliefs.

The empirical question is whether individuals change at all politically, change gradually in the years after migration, or change quickly at the time of migration. An immediate response to a change of political environment would suggest a complete reversal of the traditional political socialization perspective. Gradual change would suggest that migration acts as an agent of adult political resocialization.

Migration offers a special opportunity to examine the way individuals who have lost their immediate social supports because of geographical mobility are affected by a continuity in or change of local political environments. However, migration is a demographic phenomenon that is not well known in political science. Some time was spent filling in who migrants are and what are the main structural aspects of contemporary migration in the United States that are important to understanding migration and politics.

In Chapter 2, "A Description of Migrants," migrants and nonmigrants are contrasted and compared by their socioeconomic and political attributes. Are migrants a distinctive political group within the population, and if so, is their distinctiveness a product of their particular migration experience or their own personal attributes? The focus on their political attributes required finding out about their social and economic composition.

Migrants are different from nonmigrants, especially at the time of migration. They come from higher socioeconomic status groups in the population. Migrants, in the years after they move, tend to attain higher incomes than nonmigrants.

Politically at the time of migration, migrants appear to be less involved and committed to politics than nonmigrants. This finding may be fully explained by the relatively young age when migration is most likely to occur. Migration occurs most frequently between eighteen and thirty-five. Over time, migrants end up participating and voting in a fashion similar to that of nonmigrants. In fact, a multivariate analysis at the end of the second chapter showed that most of the variability in migrants' political participatory and electoral attributes is accounted for by the social, economic, and demographic characteristics of migrants, and not by specific migration-related attributes. The notable exception to this generalization is geographical mobility across a regional boundary.

In particular, migration to the West, the movement between the South and the North, and the shift of population within and between rural and urban areas are described in terms of the major

political characteristics of dominant social groups within each movement stream. Using the series of NES election studies made from
1952 through 1980, the composition of these movement streams and
cohorts of individual migrants were examined in Chapter 3 for signs
of change over time.

Movement to the western region of the United States was divided
into the streams stemming from the South and those from the North.
The political and socioeconomic composition of the two distinct
population streams is historically different, and that difference persists to this day. Migration from the South to the West is marked by
individuals with a lower socioeconomic status. Southerners migrating to the West tend to be Democratic and to hold political loyalties
and vote in a fashion similar to those who remained in the South.
Their Democratic inclination appears to strengthen over time after
their migration.

Migrants from the midwestern and northeastern regions of the
United States who migrated to the Far West tended to be from higher
social status groups than southern migrants and over time grew into
a population stream of increasingly higher status individuals. Politically, reflecting their higher socioeconomic status, east-to-west migrants were less Democratic upon arrival than southern in-migrants.
As a prelude to the analysis that follows, however, the Republican
tendencies of east-to-west migrants are attenuated after migration.

White migrants who moved from rural to urban areas within the
North tended to be from relatively high socioeconomic groups at the
time of migration and tended to exhibit clear upward social mobility
after migration. Politically, they were drawn from a segment of the
rural population that was at least as Republican as that of those who
remained in rural areas all their life. Over time, however, these rural-
to-urban migrants tended to be more pro-Democratic in their vote
and party identification than were those who stayed within rural
areas, but less Democratic than those who had only lived in the
urban world.

If the rural-to-urban migration originated in the South and ended
up in the North, the picture of the average migrant is different. Black
migrants growing up in the rural South and moving North are
drawn from the lower segments of the socioeconomic hierarchy, experience limited upward social mobility in the North, and get locked
into supporting the Democrats. Black migrants show a rapid increase
in level of electoral participation but remain below the level of turnout reported for indigenous northern urban blacks. Their white
counterparts are also drawn from the lower socioeconomic levels and
show only minimal status mobility after migration. Unlike blacks,

however, the whites from the South living in the North have clearly shifted their votes and their party loyalty away from the Democrats and toward the Republicans.

The urban back flow, those shifting toward a rural environment, increased in volume in the post–World War II era. The composition of this movement stream changed significantly over time as well. In the pre-1960 period migrants were largely drawn from the higher socioeconomic groups and possessed partisan attributes that reflected a more pro-Republican orientation. After 1960, however, urban-to-rural migrants were drawn from a lower status, more working-class segment of the population, which was reflected in a more pro-Democratic tendency in voting and party identification.

The second part of the book investigates the meaning and the consequences of changing local political environments. A local political environment is the sum of all external, politically relevant social or media interactions. These include personal contacts; direct contacts with elected officials, candidates, or representatives of political parties; and one-way communications from the media. The social process by which the effect of the environment is felt by the individual, I assume, is one of social contagion. Social contagion occurs when a dominant group can reinforce dominant group norms for members and project appropriate group behavior for nonmembers. The greater the degree of group homogeneity, the greater the social resonance.

The nature of political migrations is defined in terms of a proxy measure of geographical context. Election outcomes aggregated at the county or congressional district level approximate the partisan nature of local political environments. The degrees of change in local environments experienced with migration are separated into discrete categories of congruent, mixed, and incongruent change. A congruent migration occurs when an individual remains within the same type of local political environment. Incongruent migrations are those where individuals change local political environments. The likelihood of political self-selection associated with migration within and between local political environments is shown to be minimal.

I show how the current local political environment has a very strong effect on the voting behavior of migrants, even those who changed environments. This persists even when the migrant's party identification and socioeconomic and demographic attributes are controlled for statistically. Among incongruent migrants, the effect of having been exposed to a previous political environment is evident, however. Congruent migrants finally become stronger party supporters.

The party identification of migrants is influenced by the changed local political environments. Among congruent migrants, party identification appears to develop in a fashion similar to that of those who never migrated. As a group, they have strong partisan loyalties that match the nature of the local political environments in which they have resided. Incongruent migrants show a weakening of their party loyalties by exhibiting a shift in their party identification toward political independence. This shift toward independence occurs whether their previous political environment was Democratic or Republican or whether their current political environment is Democratic or Republican. Other measures of commitment to electoral politics are weakened by incongruent migration.

Some of the confounding effects on the relationship between a citizen and the local political environment are linked to family political background and age at time of migration. When migrants are arrayed both by the type of political environmental change and family partisan background, they retain the direction of family political loyalties but tend to shift their party loyalty in the direction of local political environment. This is further evidence for the weakening of party loyalties after migration.

Individuals from nonpartisan families show the least sensitivity to political environmental forces. Those from partisan split families (where mother and father hold different partisan identifications) show the greatest susceptibility to environment.

Finally, within type of family partisan background, the migrants showing the greatest degree of adaptation to the local political environment are those who possess the highest levels of political knowledge. The general conclusion remains that early family socialization is an important source of individual partisan beliefs even after migration. Yet politically homogeneous families where both parents agree in party loyalties, the type of family that appears to immunize a child from the forces of a change of political environment, have been steadily declining in recent decades.

Age related factors concern both the age at the time of migration and the length of time the individual has been exposed to a political environment. The younger the individual is when migration occurs, the greater is the eventual shift toward the local political environment. The length of exposure to the political forces of the environment is significant for the degree of adaptation. Those who have been exposed to an environmental force longer, regardless of the age they migrated, show a greater match of their party identification with the aggregate environmental partisanship.

The outcome of congruent or incongruent migration extends beyond influencing the direction of the vote or developing or retarding the strength of party identification. The ingredients that go into making a vote decision are also influenced by the type of environmental change experienced with migration. Personal economic experiences for incongruent migrants are a central component influencing their electoral decisions in both congressional and presidential elections. Their voting decision appears to depend on personal experience rather than long-term group-based loyalties such as party identification. For congruent migrants, however, the influence of personal economic rewards or losses is not a significant electoral variable. The party identification and liberal-conservative ideological orientation of congruent migrants remain central determinants of electoral decisions.

Public policy belief systems are also structured by the nature of the migration. Politically congruent migrants on average have higher levels of attitude consistency than incongruent migrants. However, when migrants' policy preferences are scrutinized for the stability of attitudes over time, a different picture emerges. Across both aggregate- and individual-level measurements of attitude stability, incongruent migrants have more stable attitudes than do congruent migrants. The difference in attitude stability between congruent migrants' belief systems and incongruent migrants' belief systems increases as the attitudes of incongruent migrants become more stable over time. A pattern of belief systems where attitude consistency is low but stability is high indicates the likelihood of personalized, idiosyncratic political beliefs. This pattern is further evidence of the development of personal orientation toward politics among incongruent migrants.

Finally, whereas incongruent migrants show both the development of personalized belief systems and reliance on self-interest for election decisions, they do not appear to be opposed to collective solutions to problems of public concern. That is, while the process of their electoral decision making is more self-reliant, incongruent migrants do not appear to become more ideologically conservative on major issues of policy.

Gradual and Unseen Micropolitical Change

A citizen's political actions and beliefs are influenced by internal migration through a slow, hard-to-see adaptation to changing local political environments. The macro manifestations result from the gradual dealignment of migrating citizens from parties. Migration is a source of progressive dissolution of the party system that can occur without institutional elites, planned political activity, or objective events.

Migration is a form of nonpolitical behavior that nearly everyone experiences. It is a self-sustaining demographic phenomenon in that it occurs at very predictable rates for decades on end. Migration is a nonpolitical act in the contemporary United States. People do not move to be near Democrats or Republicans. Most migration itself is independent of political parties, the actions of elected officials, or the major issues of public policy. And in the United States, internal migration is not linked to planned government policy.

When individuals migrate but do not change local political environments, there is no immediate apparent effect on either their voting behavior or political attitudes.

If migrants are very young, less than thirty years of age, there appears to be some diminution in party support whether or not the move is congruent or incongruent. However, over the long run, congruent migrants show a strong development of party support and voting behavior consistent with the political environments in which they have lived. Of course, it is possible that individuals who would have been only marginally identified with a party but who migrated within consonant political environments develop a stronger attachment to party because of their migration. Hence they are influenced by the political environments in which they have moved.

The net political effect of a changing political environment on migrants is to pull their vote in the direction of the new local political environment but not to convert them psychologically to a different party. The long-term consequences of an incongruent political migration are, however, not easily seen.

As we saw at the end of Chapter 4, within a five-year period there is no clear relationship between a migrant's partisanship and the environments moved from or the one entered. The effect of the move takes a great deal of time to occur. When citizens experience an incongruent migration, as we have seen, their basic political orientations change. Central to the consequences of migration is that incongruent migrants, over time and as a group, get stripped of their party identification. And without strong enduring party loyalties, they develop a personal style of political behavior. They rely upon nonpolitical experiences when they vote and form idiosyncratic belief systems when they think.

Many scholars have been concerned about the consequences of diminished partisanship. Most have suggested that both the micropolitical and the macropolitical consequences are grave (Burnham

1970). In his treatment of the normal vote Converse focused attention on those who act in the absence of party identification by assuming that such actors in the political world behave in a random fashion
(Converse 1966).

Random behavior is by definition capricious. It is action without
reason. If the roots of rational political actions are complete information and cognitive ability, random behaviors are assumed to stem
from an absence of each or both. Random political actions are actions
unconnected to the individual's political beliefs, values, or pertinent
past experiences. Traditional explanations of random political behavior have assumed that such actions result either from a lack of an
ideological structure to connect core beliefs to political behavior or
from an absence of politicized group loyalties, such as party identification. Extended party loyalties can act to connect an individual's
group interests to his or her political actions.

While particular votes and expressed attitudes of the mass public
have been assumed to be random, isolating truly random political
action is in fact difficult, especially if action is placed in context. For
actions may stem from beliefs that are the product of personalized,
idiosyncratic thinking. Actions in politics may sometimes result from
different personal and social constraints. Their cause may be unknown factors beneath the consciousness of the individual or out of
sight of the investigator (Elster 1979:135). However, taking such personal and social constraints into consideration may provide better
insight into the logic of political actions.

As we have seen, the citizen when analyzed within a partisan
context is capable of different forms of political behavior. Depending
upon his or her past contextual experience, a citizen develops a
clearly partisan orientation or a personal orientation. For citizens
who do not use group identification to make electoral decisions, decision making does not collapse or deteriorate into random actions or
thoughts. Of course, this could not have been known without measuring the nature of their past environmental experiences.

On the surface, not much appears different when citizens become
independent of party. We have seen that when the partisan context
in which voters live is considered, those who lose their partisanship
for no reason other than a migration function reasonably well. They
vote like their neighbors. They think in a systematic fashion about
policy issues. They even seem to share the policy orientations of
fellow citizens.

But beneath the surface there are differences. The actions and beliefs of these migrants appear to be individualistic and personally
directed. Policy orientations are not ordered in a consistent way to

allow for general ideological strategies to be pursued by elites. They appear instead to have an ad hoc, single-issue quality that may be important and reasonable to the individual but that also appears to be unconnected to other policy concerns.

Some in groups with weakened partisanship seem to behave in a fashion like that of the imagined rational voter. Incongruent migrants seem to use self-interest in their voting decisions. But unlike they would with a purely retrospective or prospective orientation, they appear to use self-interest to support the party tendencies of their local area as well, whether it is Democratic or Republican. They behave politically with an eye to group norms. Thus migrants when experiencing the conditions for political change seem, after a period of time, open to change and willing to change their behavior.

We have discussed a purely political side of migration. The political outcome of migration is rooted not in the economic competition of social groups but in the flow of people through partisan space. In the contemporary United States, the flow of population is politically random. Elsewhere, politics and the geographical movement of social and ethnic groups are closely tied. But everywhere, I believe, migration loosens political systems. As a result of geographical mobility, individuals become susceptible to political change and new political movements.

Unraveling the Party System

Political parties were the invention of elites. In the United States, where popular political parties first appeared, they were used to step over the local cliques and factions and to ensure that contests for Congressional seats even in remote districts were based on national issues. Parties provided an organized way to mobilize voters nationally for quadrennial presidential contests. As parties evolved, they took on a socializing role for citizens by inculcating democratic norms and support for a political system. The organizational power of a party smoothed out the differences among political skills and social and economic resources in diverse social groups.

The political advantages and disadvantages that citizens in democratic countries have stem from the social and economic inequalities that are embedded in industrial society. What the political gap in personal resources means to many fearful observers is a potential for group conflict. This potential results from blocked aspirations for personal and social betterment and from the inequality of access to a political system to secure a remedy.

For a long time it was assumed that political parties were the only institutions capable of equalizing peacefully the political aspects of the social and economic discrepancies that do exist. Where individuals lacked the personal fortunes or ability to pursue political change, parties could organize. And by collective efforts under the banner of a political party, groups attained political power in spite of their members' lack of personal resources.

The half-life of the glue holding social groups and individuals alike to political parties appears to be a function of both the length of time since the party system was formed and its success in pursuing the policy agenda that brought it into being. In the last decade, serious fluctuations in the social composition of political parties have been detected. Parties have experienced a long-term decline in their hold over the public as social groups once readily associated with a dominant party have defected to the opposition in one election after another (Petrocik 1980; Wattenberg 1984).

Most of the evidence suggesting that the public is capable of exhibiting shifts in basic political orientation comes from political behavior following epic events like wars, scandals, recessions, or depressions. More gentle sources of party system dealignment also occur as issues that originally galvanized support of a social group for a political party but that fade in importance to subsequent generations (Beck 1974). Population movement must be added to the list of personal experiences that pull citizens away from parties.

Aggregate party strength and the distribution of electoral power are not rapidly influenced by the constant movement of population. Geographical regions marked with a partisan character, like the Midwest in the 1840s or the South in the 1950s, that experience massive net in-migration do not immediately shift politically. Cities like San Francisco, Chicago, Boston, or Los Angeles that have strong partisan traditions can also maintain a political caste over decades, even in the face of large population turnover. As we have pointed out, the vote of those who change environments can change and match the receiving political environment. By weakening the individual's link to party, the simple movement of people through geopolitical spaces may continually break down the structure of group coalitions that form the bedrock of party systems.

The political effects of normal migration in normal times can not be detected from one election to another. But internal migration does influence the population's long-term political character represented by its partisanship and the ideological components of its electoral decision making. Migration alters the ability of these theoretical constructs to transform nonpolitical experiences into political reality.

Thus a proportion of migrants, even those who moved in the distant past, are likely to shift with the tide of new policy agendas and new political leadership.

For over a decade and a half, a party system realignment has been expected. It was first heralded by a civil rights movement triggered by southern racism. More predictions of a realignment were fueled by a disastrous and undeclared war in Vietnam, then by a scandal that ended a president's term of office, and then by the most serious economic recession since the Great Depression. Each event has come and gone, but much like Godot, a realignment of the political parties has not. But in the meantime, migration slowly unravels the party system.

Appendixes

Appendix A

Data, Variables, and Adjustment Procedures

Data

No single data base is sufficient for studying the political consequences of migration. In the past, scholars have mainly focused on gross migration streams, movements between north and south, east and west, or rural and urban areas. While interregional or intercommunity migrations are important sources of social or cultural change and therefore potentially important to political analysis, in this book consideration is also given to the local political environment, which may change with migration.

Data on the impact of the migrant's early political socialization in the family of origin are also essential, as are the data that focus on the age groups most likely to experience geographical mobility. Further, examination of migrants alone does not complete the picture. The nonmigrant population must also be available for a comparison with the migrating citizens. Finally, to develop a measure of political contextual change, aggregate historical evidence is used to define the migrant's past and current residential environments. Obviously no single data source or type of evidence will meet all of these requirements.

Many of the American National Election Studies (NES) from the University of Michigan's Center for Political Studies contain the minimal information needed to study the political consequences of regional or urban-rural migration over the life course. In each national election study from 1952 to 1980, data are available concerning the state and type of place in which respondents currently live, their place of birth, and the type of community in which they were raised. The more dramatic type of population movement can be examined with some care for most of the years from the 1920s to the present.

In addition, the 1970 and 1980 American National Election Studies and the 1965–1973 Youth-Parent Panel Study inquired into geographical mobility carefully enough to allow a fairly precise reconstruction of the past migratory experience for the purpose of contextual analysis. Respondents were asked the length of time they had lived in their current community. Respondents indicating that the length of time was less than all of their lives were asked the specific location (city and state) of their prior communities. In the YP panel study, each residence between 1965 and 1973 was recorded. This information helped to determine whether a move was a migration or a simple change of residence. When the information on previous residence was re-coded by county, migrants were defined as those whose current county and prior county differed. Since respondents were asked about their prior community and not their prior residence, the chance of reporting a short-hop move was considerably lessened and past changes of residence that qualified as a migration were maximized.

For the analysis of local political environments, begun in Chapter 4, the county turns out to be a politically cogent demarcation because it can be coded with historically relevant data. Other geographical units, such as regions or states, are either too large to be useful for analysis of political environmental change, or, like towns and cities, too small to have available aggregate political data comparable for the entire nation. Historical county level political data from 1900 to 1980 have been made available for the contextual coding of the 1970 and 1980 election studies and the Youth-Parent Panel Study by the Inter-University Consortium for Political and Social Research (ICPSR) of the University of Michigan.

There are three types of data that play a prominent role in the analysis. Fourteen American National Election Studies, from 1952 to 1980, formed a core time series for studying the changing composition of dominant population movement streams. The data are based on surveys of multistage area probability samples of American households in the contiguous United States. For most of the samples, the final stage is a randomized probability of the voting age of United States citizens within the household unit. Descriptions of the individual study designs and sample sizes can be obtained from the ICPSR.

In addition, two of the NES surveys, 1970 and 1980, were used for specific study of contextual effects. The 1980 studies used were the traditional preelection and postelection studies labeled C3 and C3PO and the 1980 panel studies, P1-P3. A cross-sectional sample of the voting public was interviewed initially in January and February of 1980 and then reinterviewed in person in June and September, and by telephone after the election in November. To accomplish the socialization analysis, the YP panel study was used. This study initially interviewed a sample of high school seniors in the spring of 1965 and reinterviewed them in 1973. Sampling information and panel response are contained in the codebook documentation, again distributed by the ICPSR.

Finally, a historical aggregate election data set was used to construct the partisan contextual variables used to monitor political environment. The data were originally used by Clubb, Flanigan, and Zingale (1980). A subset of these data were the county-level presidential and congressional election results from 1900 to 1978. Candidates representing third parties were precoded by whether or not they represented Democratic or Republican surrogates or were actual third parties. Major party surrogates were counted and/or combined with the two major party totals in the aggregate estimate of the vote outcome.

Variables

The original variables used in this book are documented in the NES codebooks for each study and are available through the ICPSR. This appendix describes the variables, coding conventions, and composite measures particular to this book.

Objective Social Status Index

For each year in the time series NES files, from 1952 to 1980, the education of the respondent was combined into an additive index with the objective occupational status of the head of household. A five-category index resulted. For a description of migrants, the comparison was between the two extreme high-status categories contrasted with the two lowest categories.

Subjective Social Class

The respondent's class identification is collapsed into categories of working class or middle class. Strength of class identification is ignored.

Head of Household's and Respondent's Occupational Status

The head of household's occupation is coded into four categories: professional and managerial—the highest status category; sales, lower managerial, and other white collar occupations—the second category; craftsmen and other manual blue collar operatives—the third category; and farmer—the fourth category. When used as a continuous variable, the full Duncan Socioeconomic Status Scale is used.

Education of Respondent

The education of the respondent is coded for grade school, high school, some college, college, and beyond based on the education completed. When the respondent's educational level is used as a continuous measure, the education level attained is numbered sequentially from grade one or less through advanced graduate degrees.

Family Income

The income variable is based on the respondent's family's total income before taxes. In cross-temporal categorical comparisons, the income variable is divided into quintiles.

Objective Social Status Mobility

The head of household's objective occupational status is compared to the respondent's father's or family head's occupational status. A three-category variable results in the respondent's being classified as upwardly mobile, constant, or downwardly mobile from the previous generation. When used as a continuous measure, the objective social status mobility is measured by two dummy variables, one for no mobility and one for downward mobility with upward mobility as the reference group.

Race

Race is dichotomized as black and nonblack.

Religion

Religion is separated into five groups: Catholics, Fundamental Protestant, Other Protestants, Jews, and no religion. Religion is only used in linear analysis and consists of four dummy variables with Other Protestants as the reference group.

Age Entered the Community

The number of years the respondent lived within the current community is subtracted from actual age.

Size of Originating Community

Respondents are asked whether they were brought up mostly on a farm or in the country, in a town, in a small city, in a suburb, or in a large city. The respondent's perception of the size of his or her original community is coded to a rural or urban distinction. Respondents reporting being raised on a farm or in the country are coded as rural. Everyone else is classified as urban.

Size of Current Community

The size of the current place is based on the interim surveys coded according to census data used for the national sample frame. Urban places generally are considered to be the twelve largest Standard Metropolitan Statistical Areas (SMSA), including consolidated areas and any other places classified as urban by the Census Bureau. Rural places are classified as census name locations of less than 2,500 people not within an SMSA and comprise the remaining primary sampling units. As of the 1980s urban areas are generally the two standard consolidated areas, plus the ten largest SMSAs. Rural places are those designated by the census as rural non-SMSA places with populations of less than 2,500.

Region

Four major geographical regions were used to classify migrations within the United States. New England and the Middle Atlantic states were combined for the Northeast; the east north central and west north central states were combined for the Midwest; the Solid South and the Border states were considered the South; and the Mountain and Pacific states composed the West. In Chapter 3, the North referred to the combined Northeast and Midwest. Elsewhere the West was included as a definition of North when distinctions were North and South. Regional distinctions were made for the current region, the region prior to the last migration, and the region in which the respondent grew up.

Partisanship and political commitment variables follow the standard uses commonly found in the literature. Party identification, the strength of partisanship, congressional and presidential votes, the party usually supported in presidential elections, and voting turnout are used normally. Several other political measures, however, are composite scales or indices.

Family Partisanship

This is a composite index of family partisan background. It consists of the respondent's perception of both his mother's and father's party identification. Respondents perceiving both parents as Democrats or one as Democratic and the other as apolitical or independent were coded as coming from a pro-Democratic family background. The same rule was applied to determining a pro-Republican background. Respondents having parents identifying with different political parties were coded as having a split family background. Respondents without parents, or having no recollection of both parents' partisanship, or both of whose parents were independent, apolitical, or noncitizens were coded as having a nonpartisan or apolitical family background.

Partisan Environmental Agreement

This index is the proportion of migrants who identify with the political party of their average experienced political environment.

Involvement in Politics

Psychological involvement in politics is both the respondent's concern with the outcome of the current election and his or her attention to or general interest in politics.

Extra Political Participation

Respondents are described in terms of their active forms of political participation other than voting. Working in a candidate's campaign, wearing a campaign button, attending a political rally, or any extra election-related action counts as an extra form of participation.

Political Knowledge

This is an index of factual political information such as the proportion of tax dollars that go for defense, whether or not laws can be changed without the consent of Congress, how many times a person can be elected president, the length of terms of congressmen and senators, and the party controlling the House of Representatives. The index is a summation score of correct responses.

Table A.1 shows the factor analysis used to determine the social liberalism, economic welfare, and traditionalism scales used in Chapter 7. What follows is a brief description of the scales.

Table A.1. Factor Structure of Social Liberalism, Economic Welfare, and Traditionalism

	Social Liberalism	Economic Welfare	Traditionalism
Defense spending	.37895[a]		
Aid to minorities	.56175		
Civil rights speed	.50416		
School busing	.61358		
Government services		.58128	
Inflation-unemployment		.69213	
Standard of living		.34204	
Government too powerful		.37599	
Women equal			.48802
Equal Rights Amendment			.69356
Prayer in School			.23803
Abortion			.16995

Source: American National Election Study, 1980, Pre and Post Election Surveys, Center for Political Studies, University of Michigan.
[a]Cell entries are varimax rotated factor coefficients.

Social Liberalism

This is a policy dimension based on the similarity of responses to issues of aid to minorities, the speed of civil rights, school desegregation, and the amount of defense spending. Each issue question is reported in the documentation for the 1980 NES study.

Economic Welfare

This dimension is based on the responses to policy questions concerning the current number of federal government services, the inflation versus unemployment trade-off, whether or not the federal government is too powerful, and whether the government should guarantee everyone a job and a good standard of living, and reflects the respondent's position on a general liberal to conservative continuum.

Traditionalism

A traditionalism dimension picks up a respondent's policy attitudes toward women's equality and the Equal Rights Amendment, abortion, and prayer in public schools.

Socioeconomic and Demographic Estimations

At the end of Chapter 2, Table 2.6 summarizes the results of a series of multiple regression equations aimed at estimating the effect of different aspects of migration on micropolitical attributes beyond the socioeconomic status and demographic differences that distinguish many forms of migration. Table 2.6 uses multiple correlation coefficients (R^2) and presents the differences between the estimation of variance of the political attribute explained by socioeconomic status and demographic factors in 1980 for a cross section of the population and the migrant population. In Chapters 5 and 6, linear estimations are also used to adjust and standardize observations for socioeconomic, demographic, and political biases among migrants. The adjustments take into account potential socioeconomic biases in the relationship observed between environmental change and the individual partisan attributes. The actual coefficients for these sets of equations, the standard errors of the estimates, and their significance level are available upon request from the author.

Appendix B

Local Political Environment

Several coding and analysis decisions about the construction of the local political environment variables were made in the course of the research. The aggregate time series, historical data described in Appendix A are used to measure political environmental change for the 1970 and 1980 NES surveys and the Youth-Parent survey. In all, six contextual variables were constructed to measure an individual's present and past political environments.

For each case, the reported city and state of the previous residence recorded on the interview protocol was recoded to the actual county and state. Respondents living in places outside the United States were excluded from the analysis. Partisan contexts were coded for those who changed counties of residence or who had never migrated. Both congressional and presidential election returns at the county level were used to estimate the previous political environment and the current environment at the time the individual migrated, and both county- and congressional district–level data were used to estimate the current environment at the time of the interview.

The coding for the contextual variables was conducted at UCLA in 1981 and 1982. In the NES cross-sectional studies from 1970 and 1980, the previous local political environment is the average of the returns over four congressional elections prior to an individual's migration. The current environment at the time of the migration is measured as the county average of the four congressional elections after migration. The current at the time of the interview is coded as the average of the three congressional elections prior to the interview plus the election outcome for the year in which the study was conducted. In the 1980 NES panel series, P1 wave, the current at time of the interview was for four elections prior to but not including 1980. The P1 wave began in January 1980, and hence the previous election provided a clearer fix on the nature of the environment than would one still eleven months away. The scores were in terms of the percent voting Democratic.

For congressional coding for the previous environment, if the individual moved in 1954 from Glenn County, California, to Lane County, Oregon, and was interviewed in 1980 in Lane County, the case would be coded as follows: the previous residence in Glenn County would be coded as the county's congressional outcome averaged over 1948, 1950, 1952, and 1954. The current at the time of migration would be coded for Lane County as the county's congressional outcome average for 1954, 1956, 1958, and 1960. The current at time of interview would be for 1974, 1976, 1978, and 1980.

In some areas, especially for the measure of local political environnment in the 1970 NES survey, there were series of elections (especially in the South) where congressional candidates ran unopposed, sometimes for the entire four-election series. In these cases, an effort was made to locate "faceless" candidate races, often for the state attorney general, for which the vote was reported at the county level. Such races were assumed to better represent the party vote in the area. By 1980 there were only a handful of cases that needed similar coding.

The Youth-Parent panel data presented the opportunity to measure the political consequences of migration during the transitional years from ado-lescence to early adulthood. Each of the places a respondent lived after the completion of high school is recorded in the second wave of the panel study. The age and high geographical mobility of the panel respondents prompted a slight shift in the measurement of political environment. For the purposes of establishing a meaningful local political environment, only residences lived in for six months or more are used. The political environment in the area where the respondent attended high school in 1965 is measured sepa-rately from political environments experienced after high school but prior to the current residence. The partisan concentrations of the intermediate resi-dences, those places where the respondent lived between attending high school and moving to the place in which he or she was interviewed in 1973, are averaged together. Each intermediate residence is scored with the con-gressional outcome of the county based on a four-year election average, cen-tered on the year or years in which the respondent lived in the area. This break from the environmental coding convention used for monitoring pre-vious environment in the cross-sectional election studies reflects the evi-dence that many young adults spent very short periods of time in these intermediate residences. The partisan concentration of each intermediate residence was weighted for the length of time in which the respondent lived in the locale prior to being averaged.

Calculation of the previous residence relies upon the 1965 areal concen-trations in the place where the panel respondent attended high school. The current political environment is calculated by averaging the intermediate contexts, weighted for length of time in the area, and the 1973 political envi-ronment. The 1973 contextual estimate uses the preceding four congres-sional election outcomes, beginning in 1972.

In the 1970 and 1980 NES surveys and the Youth-Parent Panel Study, presidential election outcomes are also coded as contextual variables. Two presidential elections are averaged to derive a single contextual score. The previous context and the context of the current at the time of the interview were constructed based on the average of the two preceding presidential elections. The current political environment at the time of migration was calculated according to the two presidential elections following the migra-tion.

A separate analysis of the influence of political environment based on presidential election behavior proved to be very disappointing. Presidential election contextual variables were not as useful in predicting the political attributes of migrants as were congressional outcome contextual variables. In the analysis of partisan attributes like the congressional vote, the presidential vote, party identification, or measures of political commitment, such as the strength of partisan identification, turnout, or psychological involvement; environmental measures relying solely on presidential election outcome or in partisan contextual indices that included presidential election data proved to be far less powerful predictors of political actions and beliefs than contextual measures based solely on congressional election outcomes.

Presidential election data at the county level tends to be less stable than congressional election data. From 1932 to 1980, the average year-to-year correlation for presidential elections at the county level was .188 compared to .347 for congressional election data. Even breaking the time series into shorter periods does not alter this pattern. Presidential elections are subject to far more national short-term forces than are congressional elections, and even though the aggregate vote is partially explained by the relative concentrations of partisans, it does not provide as useful a fix on the partisan environment as elections reflecting the local forces, such as congressional races.

Appendix C

Probability Model of Environmental Effects

Suppose that political environment is measured as the percent of all the votes received by one party, the Democratic, D, from congressional elections held in one place between 1974 to 1980. The average percent supporting party D is a product of both the actions of members, M_j, of party D, and nonmembers $(1 - M_j)$. This can be expressed as

$$< 1 > \quad \overline{D} = O_1 M_j + O_2 (1 - M_j).$$

The coefficients, O_1, O_2, are rates of support. They can be used to represent social resonance and behavioral contagion. But regarding the contextual effects obtained with the aggregate areal partisan averages, the forms contextual variables take depend upon the assumed social process underlying the effect. Suppose that members and nonmembers in an environment are assumed to be differentially affected by the context. Under the social resonance assumption, members of party D are more influenced by context than nonmembers. The following represents the two rates of support:

$$< 2 > \quad O_1 = p_1 + p_2 M_j$$

$$< 3 > \quad O_2 = p_3.$$

Here, p_2 represents the reinforcement of the propensity to behave based on group social interaction within the environment, and p_1 and p_3 represent individual-level behavior independent of environment. When equations $< 2 >$ and $< 3 >$ are substituted into equation $< 1 >$, the following model can be expressed:

$$< 4 > \quad \overline{D} = p_3 + (p_1 - p_3)M_j + p_2(M_j{}^2).$$

Under this model, if the context is dominated by one social group, then the average political behavior of the area would be the result of the normal level of partisan support, plus the difference between the individual predispositions of members and nonmembers, given the proportion of the population that are within the dominant group. The final term is the impact of members' interaction with each other.

But if, as Erbring and Young (1979) suggest, behavior depends upon surrounding behavior, and not just upon the social composition of a context, then both members and nonmembers are likely to be influenced by the environmental forces. That condition can be represented by the following set of expressions:

$$< 5 > \quad O_1 = p_1 + p_2\overline{D}$$

$$< 6 > \quad O_2 = p_2 + p_4\overline{D}.$$

When equations $< 5 >$ and $< 6 >$ are substituted into equation $< 1 >$, the resulting model is

$$< 7 > \quad \overline{D} = \frac{p_3 + (p_1 - p_3)M_j}{1 - p_4 + (p_4 - p_2)M_j}.$$

In this model, the average level of support given a party is the ratio of individual- to group-based effects for members *and* nonmembers alike. In the case of this study, the members are partisans supporting one or the other political party. And the outcome contextual variable is the result of actions of both classes of partisans.

The basic probability model underlying a social contagion process can now be stated formally. (The models that follow are extensions of several presented by Likens and Kohfeld 1980.)

Let

    Model I: Simple individual effects
    Model II: Simple contextual effects
    Model III: Multiple individual and contextual effects

Let

    R_t = proportion of the mass public Republican at time t.

$$< 1 > \quad \Delta R_t = R_{t+1} - R_t$$

Model I: Rational calculus

$$< 2 > \quad \Delta R_t = p_1 (A - R_t) - p_6 (R_t - B)$$

where

        $B \leqslant R_t \leqslant A$
        $0 \leqslant p_1, p_6 \leqslant 1$

            A = proportion of population who are unchangeable Democrats

B = proportion of population who are unchangeable Republicans

$A - R_t$ = Democratic population who are potential Republicans

$R_t - B$ = Republicans who are potential Democrats

p_1 = probability that a Democrat will become a Republican

p_6 = probability that a Republican will become a Democrat

Simplifying

$<3>$ $R_{t+1} = (1 - p_1 - p_6)R_t + (p_1A + p_6B)$.

When $<2>$ is set $= 0$, the equilibrium point for R becomes

$<4>$ $R_e = (p_1A + p_6B) / (p_1 + p_6)$.

Model II: Under the constraints of contextual behavior, a model of partisan behavior becomes:

$<5>$ $\Delta R_t = C_1(A - R_t) - C_2(R_t - B)$

where

$<6>$ $C_1 = p_2R_t - p_3p_2 (1 - R_t)R_t$

$<7>$ $C_2 = p_4 (1 - R_t) - p_5p_4R_t (1 - R_t)$

and

p_2 = probability that a Democrat becomes a Republican due to exposure to other Republicans

p_3 = probability that a Democrat remains a Democrat due to exposure to other Democrats

p_4 = probability that a Republican becomes a Democrat due to exposure to other Democrats

p_5 = probability that a Republican remains a Republican due to exposure to other Republicans.

Simplifying

$<8>$ $R_{t+1} = B_3R_t^3 + B_2R_t^2 + B_1R_t + \alpha$

$$< 9 > \quad B_2 = p_2p_3 - p_2 + p_2p_3A + p_4 + p_4p_5 + p_4p_5B$$

$$< 10 > \quad B_1 = p_2A - p_2p_3A - p_4 - p_4B - p_4p_5B + 1$$

$$< 11 > \quad B_3 = p_5p_4 - p_3p_2$$

$$< 12 > \quad \alpha = p_4B.$$

Model III: Individual and social effect

$$< 13 > \quad \Delta R_t = w_iI_t + w_sS_t$$

I_t and S_t are given already in Model I, II as,

$$< 14 > \quad I_t = p_1 (A - R_t) - p_6 (R_t - B)$$

$$< 15 > \quad S_t = (p_2R_t - p_3 (1 - R_t) p_2R_t (A - R_t) - $$
$$(p_2 (1 - R_t) - p_5R_tp_4 (1 - R_t) (R_t - B).$$

Simplification

$$< 16 > \quad R_{t+1} = B_3R_t^3 + B_2R_t^2 + B_1R_t + \alpha$$

$$< 17 > \quad B_3 = (-p_2p_3 + p_4p_5) w_i$$

$$< 18 > \quad B_2 = (p_2p_3 - p_2 + p_2p_3A + p_4p_5 + p_4 + p_4p_5B)w_s$$

$$< 19 > \quad B_1 = (p_2A - p_2p_3A - p_4 - p_4B - p_4p_5B)w_s + (-p_1 - p_6)w_i$$
$$< 20 > \quad\quad = (p_4B)w_s + (p_1A + p_6B)w_i$$

where $w_i + w_s = 1.$

Recall Model II: Contextual behavior

In C let the probability of a Democrat's becoming a Republican as a result of exposure to one Republican be

$$< 21 > \quad p_2 = p_cp_r$$

where

> p_c = probability that a Democrat has contact with one Republican
>
> p_r = probability that as a result of such contact there is a conversion from Democrat to Republican
>
> N = number of people in environment
>
> $n = RN$ = number of people who are Republicans in a given environment of size N.

Probability of a Democrat becoming a Republican given exposure to two Republicans:

$$< 22 > \quad p_2 = (1 - (1 - p_c)^2)p_r$$

Probability of multiple Democrats becoming Republican given a population of size N:

$$< 23 > \quad p_2 = (1 - (1 - p_c)^{R_t N})p_r(1 - R_t)$$

In an environment with a "known n" Model II,

$$< 24 > \quad \Delta R_t = (p_2 R_t - p_3 (1 - R_t) p_2 R_t) (A - R_t) - \\ p_2 (1 - R_t) - p_5 R_t p_4 (1 - R_t) (R_t - B)$$

becomes under a nonlinear contextual measure

$$< 25 > \quad R_{t+1} = [(1 - (1 - p_{2c}) R_t N)p_{2r} (1 - R_t)]R_t \\ [(1 - (1 - p_{3c}) (1 - R_t N) p_{3r} R_t (1 - R_t)] \\ [(1 - (1 - p_{2c}) R_t N) p_{2r} (1 - R_t)]R_t (A - R_t) \\ \text{etc.}$$

Notes

Chapter 1

1. To Durkheim the environment was the foundation of the social laws of nature, which were "ways of acting, thinking, and feeling that present the noteworthy property of existing outside the individual conscious. These types of conduct or thoughts are not only external to the individual but are, moreover, endowed with coercive power, by virtue of which they impose themselves upon him, independent of his individual will" (1951:301). For an excellent review of the macrosociological implications of context, see Laczko n.d.

2. The separate effect of environmental variables is sometimes called a breakage effect, a quaint reference to the custom of bookies' keeping the money left over as the result of rounding off winnings. The notion of breakage implies a minor, secondary effect. It will not be used in this analysis.

3. Chapter 4 discusses in detail three aspects of a local political environment: personal networks, direct political contacts, and the mass media, and sets out the logic for understanding the operations and measurement of political environmental change central to the later analysis. Appendix C presents a more formal treatment of the way in which environmental change induces micro effects and develops specific propositions and their political consequences. In Appendix C, I outline likely micro processes, resonance and social contagion, which cause an individual to adapt to a new environment after migration. It is sufficient to note here that there is a literature on environmental effects in both the biological and the social sciences (Levin 1961; May 1974, 1976; Cohen 1978; Sprague and Westefield 1979a).

4. At the macro level, a lack of political immunization has been associated with a party system change that occurs during a period of realignment. Andersen (1979) and Petrocik (1980) suggest that past party realignments stem from the biased mobilization of the politically unimmunized: previous nonvoters such as the young, new immigrants and their children, or formerly disenfranchised blacks. Thus the realignment of the 1930s, for example, may not have resulted from a conversion of Republicans to Democrats but rather from the selective recruitment into the Democratic ranks of those eligible but previously inactive (Andersen 1979:chaps. 3–4; Petrocik n.d. In

addition, political realignments in various regions of the country in the 1850s and 1890s seem also to have resulted from a biased mobilization of new voters. Groups of new voters often aligned themselves politically in ways which were not relevant to the older members of the electorate. Petrocik states that in the 1890s newer members within certain regions, immigrants in many cases, or the young, produced the bulk of the observed change in the electoral system (Petrocik, 1980).

Chapter 2

1. The local political environments in which the individual lived can be reconstructed retroactively with historical political information available at the county level. Appendix A describes the data used in this and subsequent chapters. Appendix B describes the construction of local political environments.

2. These data are also described in Appendix A.

3. For description of the political variables, see Appendix A.

4. Briefly, dummy variables, when included in multiple regression equations, use the category of each nominal level variable as a new variable by creating k dummy vectors, where k is the number of categories minus one. The inclusion of all dummies created from a given nominal variable would produce an insolvable normal equation since the k(th) dummy variable would be completely determined by the first k-1 dummies entered into the equation. The dummy variable is coded in a binary fashion to yield dichotomous variables for which an attribute is either present in the model or absent. For instance, if the purpose of the equation is to test the effect of migration or nonmigration on political attributes the model would appear as follows:

$$Y = B'X + B'D + E$$

where

Y = a vector of political attributes

X = a vector of socioeconomic, demographic, and age attributes

D = dummy variable (0 = migrant; 1 = nonmigrant)

B = vector of regression coefficients.

In the above equation, D tests the presence (or absence) of an effect of migration by treating the vector of 1s and 0s as a continuous, independent measure in the regression equations. Other migration experiences can also be constructed in a similar manner by the use of dummy variables. In Table 2.6, the distance of the migration, community size change, regional mobility and region by community size mobility are substituted in different equations to measure the unique effect of a specific migration experience.

5. In addition, race and religious identification were used as independent variables. Age, occupational mobility, race, and religion are constructed as

dummy variables. While it is common to bend the assumptions of linear models to gain the extra explanatory power from the procedure, certain steps can be taken to minimize the discrepancy between the assumptions of the statistical models and the variables used. The independent variables underlying the estimates of Table 2.6 are either continuous, interval level or nominal and constructed for the purposes of the analysis as dummy variables. The age and socioeconomic status independent variables are similar though not identical to the categorical socioeconomic or age variables used at the beginning of the chapter to describe migrants. Several of the socioeconomic factors are variables that are intercorrelated. As a consequence, multicollinearity may influence the estimate of the model. When independent variables are highly interrelated, the variances of the estimated coefficients for the independent variables will be biased as a result of increased sensitivity to random errors, and might therefore yield unstable estimates. This condition is only a problem when there is an attempt to estimate the separate effects of each of the linearly dependent predictors. Multicollinearity does not affect the other predictors in the equation that are not collinear, nor does it affect the overall predictive power of the model. The central concern of this analysis is to determine the impact that the migration experience has on important individual political characteristics above and beyond the effect of socioeconomic factors. In the summaries of the various equations the overestimation by some nonpolitical variables does not hamper the analysis.

6. Within the set of equations not reported here, significant coefficients for the migration status variables were found for the migrant's level of psychological involvement in politics. Significant coefficients were also found for interregional migration for strength of party identification, presidential vote, and congressional vote. The other measures of migration experience were not significant for the selected political attributes, given the migrant's socioeconomic status and demographic profile.

Chapter 3

1. According to the Taeubers, from the 1900s on, the Mountain and Pacific states of the West grew, in absolute terms, faster than any other region. When it first appeared in the census returns in the 1850s, the population of the West was about 179,000. In every decade other than the 1890s, it grew at double or triple the rate of the rest of the country. Thus while the rest of the country increased in population 6 times between 1850 and 1890, the West grew 110 times (Taeuber and Taeuber 1958:15). The data for Figure 3.1 from 1870 to 1970 were taken from Taeuber (1972). The 1980 data were from the U.S. Bureau of the Census (1983).

2. The Objective Social Status Index is a composite of the respondent's education and the head of household's occupation. The index yields six ranks from higher to lower social status. The entries in Figure 3.1, and in other tables throughout the chapter, are scores from a Percentage Difference Index (PDI). Calculating the PDI score is straightforward. For the Objective Social Status Index, the PDI score is the proportion in the top two status groups minus the proportion in the bottom two for each migration stream. The full range of the index is from +100, which would indicate that all migrants are high-status individuals, to 0, which would indicate that there is

a balance between high- and low-status migrants in the stream, to −100, which would mean that all migrants are lower status.

3. When blacks are excluded from the south-west migration stream, the PDI score for the Objective Social Status Index is −37 in the pre-1960 period and −35 after 1960.

4. The West includes the Mountain and Pacific states of Arizona, Colorado, Idaho, Montana, Nevada, New Mexico, Utah, Wyoming, California, Oregon, and Washington. Alaska and Hawaii are excluded. The South includes in this analysis the Solid South and Border states of Alabama, Arkansas, Florida, Georgia, Louisiana, Mississippi, North Carolina, South Carolina, Texas, Virginia, Kentucky, Maryland, Oklahoma, Tennessee, Washington, D.C., and West Virginia; the North encompasses New England, the Middle Atlantic states, and the east and west north central states.

A native population consists of those who in the year of the survey were interviewed in the region of birth. A small percent include return migrants who left their region of origin and subsequently returned. The National Election Studies (NES) surveys taken between 1952 and 1980, however, do not allow for a complete mapping of the residential history of respondents.

5. For example, in the western states, over 90 percent of the cities use ballots for local elections which do not identify the party of the candidate. Outside of the West, less than 60 percent of the cities use nonpartisan ballots in their elections (Hawley 1973:14–18).

6. See Appendix A for the classification of urban and rural places used in this section.

Chapter 4

1. Perhaps no two authors mean exactly the same things by context and environment. I prefer to use the term *political environment* in this book, though I consider the term *political context* to carry the same meaning. In the sections that review the work of other scholars, however, I have used whichever term they use in the work being discussed.

2. Formally, an ecological niche is defined as "a region of n-dimensional hyper-space, comparable to the phase-space of statistical mechanics" (Hutchinson 1944).

3. Again, a formal statement of the political implications of contextual change is presented but not tested in Appendix C.

4. Without some degree of psychological immunity, the functional form of contagion should be logistic. If immunity exists, it modifies the spread within an environment due to contagion. An analogy is the degree of illness associated with contagion. Some people get so sick they die, whereas others get more mild forms of the illness, depending upon their immunity, the strain of the illness, and other factors. Another problem, of course, is how to sort out the effects of context based on behavioral measures similar to the dependent phenomena they are designed to explain. In contextual analysis this is quite appropriate (Boyd and Iversen 1979). The analyses in the subsequent chapters explain congressional and presidential voting, partisan identification and the strength of attraction to parties as a function of the influence of partisan context, and additional individual-level social and political explanatory variables.

5. In several cases migrants relocated immediately after the 1930s realignment. Differences between their current and previous political environments may be greater than expected based on the macropolitical change associated with a major party realignment. In other instances especially in the South, there were no congressional races. Statewide races, such as attorney general, were substituted for congressional elections.

6. The measure of current local political environment at the time the individual migrates is a useful variable for several reasons. It can be used to determine the amount of external change or continuity in a political environment from a time point in the past when the individual first entered the new area to the time his or her political traits were measured. Thus the measure of current political environment at the time of migration is useful for smoothing over fluctuations of the current political environment over time. In the subsequent analysis, the estimation of a migrant's current political environment will be based on the average percent voting Democratic in the current area at the time of the migration and at the time of the interview.

7. It should be stressed that the *incongruent* category includes those who have moved from dominant to competitive areas. Empirical investigations show that those who have experienced such change behave just like those who have migrated to an environment dominated by the opposition. The reason follows from the assumption about contextual effects. Those who earlier had lived in a dominated political milieu and are currently in a competitive setting have had the uniformity of political cues broken by migration. On the other hand, those moving from competitive to dominated political environments are not as unsettled by migration because they have had previously received information about, and presumably have had contact with, *both* political parties.

8. A county or congressional district is assumed to be dominated by a political party when an average of at least 55 percent voted for the congressional candidate in the respective years used to compile the current or previous partisan contextual measure. A Republican environment, therefore, has less than 45 percent voting for a Democratic congressional candidate, whereas a Democratic environment has at least 55 percent voting for the Democratic candidate. A competitive environment is defined as a county or congressional district with between 46 and 54 percent voting for the Democratic candidate.

Chapter 5

1. Multiple regression equations of the vote variables were constructed with party identification, demographic and socioeconomic variables as predictors. From the estimated equations, a comparison can be made between the average expected vote and the average actual vote within the category of partisan contextual change (Theil 1971:111–24). The equation used to generate the expected vote was as follows:

$$EV = OV - (b_i ZX_i) - (b_j ZX_j) - \ldots - (b_n ZX_n) - a + \overline{OV}$$

where

EV = the resultant score on the adjusted variable for any given migrant

OV = unadjusted vote for any given migrant

b_{ij} . . . n = regression weight for the corresponding independent variable for which OV is being adjusted

ZX_{ij} . . . n = the migrant's standardized score on the ith jth, independent variable

a = constant

$\overline{OV}$ = mean of OV.

2. Because of the relationship between the age of the migrant and the length of time in the current environment, the impact of age as well as other social and demographic factors has been removed and reported as Adjusted Mean Difference at the bottom of Table 5.2. The correlation between age and the length of time in the current environment is high. To remove the effects of this age bias, a series of linear adjustments of the migrant's party identification scores was performed. The respondents' current age, socioeconomic status and mobility, subjective social class, income, education, and current region were included in a multiple regression model predicting their party identification. The scores in Table 5.2 are the standardized residuals of this estimation procedure.
3. The issue of the direct effect of self-interest is taken up in Chapter 7.

Chapter 6

1. This does not imply that political values were not transmitted to southern black children prior to the civil rights movement. Obviously the extent to which the civil rights movement mobilized black youth during the 1950s and the early 1960s suggests that southern black youth were inculcated with definite political norms and values, most probably by their parents, schools, and church. Yet it is questionable that *partisan* values were important (Marvick 1965).
2. In fact, Jennings and Niemi rather clearly showed that in determining the child's partisan outlook, mothers hold a slight edge when they are in disagreement with their husbands. But because of the limited number of migrants and the small size of the split partisan background variable, this point is ignored.
3. The 1965–1973 Youth-Parent Panel (YP) data, one of the data sets used in this chapter, are described in Appendix A. Evidence of the political effects of migrants' family background is also present from 1970 and 1980 NES studies. The YP panel data provide an excellent source for determining from how early family socialization persists when migrants confront changing political environments. The Youth-Parent Panel Study paid close attention to the residential mobility of young adults. The study asked reinterviewed respondents where they had lived between 1965 and 1973. Those who are familiar with the richness of the YP panel study might well wonder why the

actual partisan composition of the family as measured from the subsample of interviews with both parents is not used to determine family partisan composition rather than the child's perceptions in 1965. The problem is one of reduced cases. The proportion of both parents interviewed, one-third out of the original parent sample, and the proportion of *their* children who migrated by the age of twenty-six, about half of the one-third, produces too few observations. A slightly higher proportion of migrants report a more homogeneous partisan family background than actually exists based on the partisanship reported by both parents. The following results in this chapter should be interpreted given this caveat.

4. See Appendix B for the way in which political environment was coded for the YP panel data.

5. In Figure 6.1 both the YP panel data and the 1980 NES data are used to show how early family political socialization influences adult party identification. Within the category of parental partisanship, the mean partisanship of young migrants from the YP panel study is first shown as it was in their late adolescence as monitored in 1965, prior to migration. A second entry shows their average party identification after migration as measured in 1973. The panel migrants are distinguished by their environmental experience in Democratic or Republican categories, depending upon the party dominating the local milieu. To provide continuity with the previous chapters and to add validity to the YP panel study, the data from the 1980 NES survey are also examined.

6. Again, Appendix A provides a list of the items used in the construction of the political knowledge index and the manner in which they are combined into a single measure. Questions about political information were included in both the YP panel study and in the 1970 NES.

7. Even more than with other analyses conducted for this study, nonpolitical variables like education, occupational status, and subjective social class may distort. Education especially should be linked to the abilities a person has to understand and to use political information in an electoral setting. This could be the result of formal education or relative position in the social structure. The better educated, higher status population has been repeatedly shown to be more concerned with politics and more personally involved in the political process (Verba and Nie 1972). These are also individuals who can reason about politics in the most abstract and ideological fashion, and whose knowledge about politics, parties, and candidates is apt to be based on a knowledge of issues of public policy (Carmines and Stimson 1980:85–86). In this case age and age-related factors may confound inferences made from political knowledge in that older migrants may have been exposed to politics for far greater periods of time and consequently know more about the political world. Moreover, it is possible that a higher level of knowledge of political facts implies a greater individual cognitive capacity to deal with abstract politics without the cues provided by social groups or political parties. As such, the source of adjustment to environmental forces may once again rest on the demographic and social characteristics of the individual migrant. Again these factors must be considered in assessing the degree to which political knowledge works in conjunction with or against political environmental experience to alter or retain the partisan attributes generated in the family.

Chapter 7

1. See Appendix A for the construction of these issue scales. Based upon a factor analysis of respondents' answers to twenty issues of public policy, a varimax rotated solution yielded seven dimensions. The first three were used in this analysis because they account for the majority of the variance and represent the type of issues that dominated the elections of 1980.

2. The 1980 NES data contain not only the standard pre- and post-election surveys, but also a panel study conducted over the entire election year. For those who have migrated in previous years, this phase of the 1980 study provides a way of examining the stability of key political attitudes over a relatively homogeneous time period. See Appendix A for a description of the 1980 panel data used. Again, the same partisan contextual variables used in the cross-sectional samples from 1980 and 1970 NES data the YP panel data were added to the 1980 (P1) wave migrants.

3. An individual measure of attitude stability is an extension of the method proposed by Barton and Parsons (1977) and Wyckoff (1980). First each respondent's issue position is standardized according to the average response and standard deviation of the total population within a panel wave. Then the standardized responses of each panel respondent are summed and then divided by the total number of responses each gave to a given issue across the panel. This result is an average standardized stability score. A final calculation is done to determine the deviation of each respondent away from this standardized panel average. The following calculation formula is used to derive the score:

$$S_j = \left[\frac{\sum\limits_{i=1}^{n} (I_{ij} - \overline{I}_j)^2}{N} \right]^{1/2}$$

where

S_j = stability score for each individual
I_{ij} = standardized response on issue for each respondent
$\overline{I}_j$ = average standard score for n issues responses
N = number of times j responded to an issue within the panel.

The final measure, S_j, is the deviation of the individual's response to an issue average from his standardized average response. As S_j approaches the value zero, the respondent shows higher levels of individual stability.

Bibliography

Abramson, Paul R. 1972. "Intergenerational Social Mobility and Partisan Choice." *American Political Science Review* 66:1291–94.

Allais, M. 1953. "Le comportement de l'homme rationnel devant le risque: Critique des postulats et axioms de l'école americaine." *Econometrica* 21:503–46.

Alvord, Clarence W., and Lee Bidgood. 1912. *First Exploration in the Trans-Allegheny Region by Virginians, 1650–1694*. Cleveland: Arthur H. Clark.

Alwin, Dwaine F. 1976. "Assessing School Effects: Some Identities." *Sociology of Education* 49:294–303.

Andersen, Kristi. 1979. *The Creation of a Democratic Majority 1928–1936*. Chicago: University of Chicago Press.

Anderson, T. R. 1955. "Intermetropolitan Migration: A Comparison of the Hypotheses of Zipf and Stouffer." *American Sociological Review* 20:287–91.

Attenborough, David. 1979. *Life on Earth*. Boston: Little, Brown and Co.

Barton, Allen H., and R. Wayne Parsons. 1977. "Measuring Belief System Structure." *Public Opinion Quarterly* 41:159–80.

Beck, Paul Allen. 1974. "A Socialization Theory of Partisan Realignment." In *The Politics of Future Citizens: New Dimensions in the Political Socialization of Children*, edited by Richard G. Niemi, pp. 199–219. San Francisco: Jossey-Bass.

———. 1977. "Partisan Dealignment in the Postwar South." *American Political Science Review* 71:477–96.

Bennett, W. Lance. 1975. *The Political Mind and the Political Environment*. Lexington: Heath, Lexington Books.

Berelson, Bernard R., Paul F. Lazarsfeld, and William N. McPhee. 1954. *Voting*. Chicago: University of Chicago Press.

Berliner, Joseph S. 1977. "Internal Migration: A Comparative Disciplinary View." In *Internal Migration: A Comparative Perspective*, edited by Alan A. Brown and Egon Neuberger, pp. 443–61. New York: Academic Press.

Bernard, William S. 1969. "Interrelationships between Migrants and Negroes." *International Migration Review* 3:47–57.

Birbeck, Morris. 1818. *Notes on a Journey in America, from the Coast of Virginia to the Territory of Illinois*. London: Severn and Co.

Bishop, Barbara R., and Linda Beckman. 1971. "Developmental Confor-
     mity." *Developmental Psychology* 5:536.
Blau, Peter, and O. Dudley Duncan. 1967. *The American Occupational Struc-
     ture*. New York: John Wiley.
Bloom, Howard S., and H. Douglas Price. 1975. "Voter Response to Short-
     term Economic Conditions: The Asymmetric Effect of Prosperity and Re-
     cession." *American Political Science Review* 69:1240–54.
Blumberg, Leonard, and R. Bell. 1959. "Urban Migration and Kinship Ties."
     Social Problems 6:328–33.
Bodenhofer, Hans-Joachim. 1967. "The Mobility of Labor and the Theory of
     Human Capital." *Journal of Human Resources* 2:431–48.
Bogue, Donald J., and Warren S. Thompson. 1949. "Migration and Dis-
     tance." *American Sociological Review* 14:236–44.
Boyd, Richard H., Jr., and Gudmund R. Iversen. 1979. *Contextual Analysis:
     Concepts and Statistical Techniques*. Belmont: Wadsworth Publishing Co.
Brim, Orville G., Jr., and S. Wheeler. 1966. *Socialization After Childhood: Two
     Essays*. New York: John Wiley.
Brown, Alan A., and Egon Neuberger, eds. 1977. *Internal Migration: A Com-
     parative Perspective*. New York: Academic Press.
Brown, James S., George A. Hillery, and Gordon DeJong. 1965. "Migration
     Systems of the Southern Appalachians: Some Demographic Observa-
     tions." *Rural Sociology* 30:33–48.
Brown, Thad A. 1974. "The Political Consequences of Population Movement
     and Population Dispersal." Unpublished paper, University of Michigan.
————. 1977. "Some Individual Political Consequences of Migration in the
     United States." Ph.D. diss., University of Michigan.
————. 1981. "On Contextual Change and Partisan Attributes." *British Jour-
     nal of Political Science* 11:427–47.
————. 1987. "The Migrant's Clock: Modeling Assimilation Dynamics in
     Backward Recurrence Times." Unpublished paper, University of Mis-
     souri-Columbia.
Budge, Ian, Ivor Crew, and Dennis Farlie, eds. 1976. *Party Identification and
     Beyond: Representations of Voting and Party Competition*. London: John Wi-
     ley.
Burk, Arthur S. 1977. *Cause, Chance, and Reason: An Inquiry into the Nature of
     Scientific Evidence*. Chicago: University of Chicago Press.
Burnham, Walter Dean. 1970. *Critical Elections and the Mainsprings of Ameri-
     can Politics*. New York: W.W. Norton & Co.
Butler, David, and Donald Stokes. 1976. *Political Change in Britain*. College
     ed. New York: St. Martin's Press.
Cain, Bruce E., John A. Ferejohn, and Morris P. Fiorina. 1984. "The Con-
     stituency Service Basis of the Personal Vote for U.S. Representatives and
     British MPs." Working Paper in Political Science no. P-84-1. Stanford:
     The Hoover Institution.
Calvert, Randall L., and John A. Ferejohn. 1983. "Coattail Voting in Recent
     Presidential Elections." *American Political Science Review* 77:407–19.
Campbell, Angus. 1971. *White Attitudes Toward Black People*. Ann Arbor: In-
     stitute for Social Research Publication.
Campbell, Angus, Philip E. Converse, and Willard L. Rodgers. 1976. *The
     Quality of American Life*. New York: Russell Sage Foundation.

Campbell, Angus, Philip E. Converse, Warren E. Miller, and Donald E. Stokes. 1960. *The American Voter*. New York: John Wiley.

Carmines, Edward G., and James A. Stimson. 1980. "The Two Faces of Issue Voting." *American Political Science Review* 74:78–91.

Carrothers, G. A. P. 1956. "A Historical Review of the Gravity and Potential Concepts of Human Interaction." *Journal of American Institutional Planners* 2:94–102.

Chamberlain, Neil W., Donald E. Cullen, and David Lewin. 1980. *The Labor Sector*. 3d ed. New York: McGraw-Hill.

Clarke, Peter, and Susan H. Evans. 1983. *Covering Campaigns: Journalism in Congressional Elections*. Stanford: Stanford University Press.

Clubb, Jerome M., William H. Flanigan, and Nancy H. Zingale. 1980. *Partisan Realignment: Voters, Parties, and Government in American History*. Beverly Hills: Sage Publications.

Cohen, Joel. 1978. *Food Webs and Niche Space*. Princeton: Princeton University Press.

Cole, Cyrenus. 1938. *I Am a Man: The Indian Black Hawk*. Iowa City: Iowa State Historical Society.

Converse, Philip E. 1964. "The Nature of Belief Systems in Mass Publics." In *Ideology and Discontent*, edited by D. E. Apter, pp. 206–61. New York: Free Press.

———. 1966. "The Concept of the Normal Vote." In *Elections and the Political Order*, edited by A. Campbell, P. E. Converse, W. E. Miller, and D. E. Stokes, pp. 9–39. New York: John Wiley.

———. 1970. "Attitudes and Non-Attitudes: Continuation of a Dialogue." In *The Quantitative Analysis of Social Problems*, edited by E. R. Tufte, pp. 168–89. Reading: Addison-Wesley.

Converse, Philip E., and Gregory B. Markus. 1979. "Plus ça change . . . : The New CPS Election Study Panel." *American Political Science Review* 73:32–49.

Converse, Philip E., Warren E. Miller, J. Gerald Rusk, and Arthur C. Wolfe. 1969. "Continuity and Change in American Politics: Parties and Issues in the 1968 Election." *American Political Science Review* 63:1083–105.

Cox, Kevin R. 1974. "The Spatial Structuring of Information and Partisan Attitudes." In *Social Ecology*, edited by Mattei Dogan and Stein Rokkan, pp. 157–85. Cambridge, Mass.: MIT Press.

Crotty, William J., and Gary C. Jacobson. 1980. *American Parties in Decline*. Boston: Little, Brown and Co.

Davies, James C. 1963. *Human Nature in Politics: The Dynamics of Political Behavior*. New York: John Wiley.

Dawson, Richard E., Kenneth Prewitt, and Karen S. Dawson. 1977. *Political Socialization*. Boston: Little, Brown and Co.

Doddridge, Philip. 1783. "Notes on the Early Settlement and Indian Wars of the Western Part of Virginia and Pennsylvania from the Year 1763 until the Year 1783 Inclusive."

Dogan, Mattei. 1967. "Political Cleavages and Social Stratification in France and Italy." In *Party Systems and Voter Alignments: Cross-National Perspectives*, edited by S. M. Lipset and S. Rokkan, pp. 129–95. New York: Free Press.

Durkheim, Emile. 1951. *Suicide*. Glencoe, Ill.: Free Press.

Easterlin, Richard A. 1980. "American Population Since 1940." In *The American Economy in Transition*, edited by Martin Feldstein, pp. 275–321. Chicago: University of Chicago Press.

Easton, David, and Jack Dennis. 1969. *Children in the Political System*. Chicago: University of Chicago Press.

Eldersveld, Samuel J. 1982. *Political Parties in American Society*. New York: Basic Books.

Eldridge, Hope J. 1964. "A Cohort Approach to the Analysis of Migration Differentials." *Demography* 1:212–19.

Elster, Jon. 1979. *Ulysses and the Sirens: Studies in Rationality and Irrationality*. New York: Cambridge University Press.

Epstein, Leon O. 1958. *Politics in Wisconsin*. Madison: University of Wisconsin Press.

Erbring, Lutz, and Alice A. Young. 1979. "Individual and Social Structure: Contextual Effects as Endogenous Feedback." *Sociological Methods and Research* 7:396–430.

Fairchild, Charles K. 1969. "Transfer of Population from Rural to Urban Areas: Rural Disadvantaged Mobility." Paper presented at the annual spring meeting of the Industrial Relations Research Association, Madison, Wis.

Farkas, George. 1974. "Specification, Residuals and Contextual Effects." *Sociological Methods and Research* 2:333–63.

Featherman, David L., and Robert M. Hauser. 1978. *Opportunity and Change*. New York: Academic Press.

Ferman, Louis A., and Michael Aiken. 1967. "Mobility and Situational Factors in the Adjustment of Older Workers to Job Displacement." *Human Organization* 26:235–41.

Festinger, Leon. 1957. *A Theory of Cognitive Dissonance*. Evanston, Ill.: Row, Peterson.

Fiorina, Morris P. 1977. "The Case of the Vanishing Marginals: The Bureaucracy Did It." *American Political Science Review* 71:177–81.

———. 1981. *Retrospective Voting in American National Elections*. New Haven: Yale University Press.

Fitzpatrick, Joseph P. 1966. "The Importance of 'Community' in the Process of Immigrant Assimilation." *International Migration Review* 1:5–7.

Folger, John. 1953. "Some Aspects of Migration in the Tennessee Valley." *American Sociological Review* 18:253–60.

Ford, Henry V. 1915. *The Scotch-Irish in America*. Princeton: Princeton University Press.

Furniss, George M. 1969. "The Political Assimilation of Negroes in New York City." Ph.D. diss., Columbia University.

Goodman, Leo A. 1961. "Modifications of the Dorn-Stouffer-Tibbits Method For 'Testing the Significance of Comparisons in Sociological Data.'" *American Journal of Sociology* 66:355–63.

Goodrich, Carter, et al. 1936. *Migration and Economic Opportunity*. Philadelphia: University of Pennsylvania Press.

Greenstein, Fred I. 1965. *Children and Politics*. New Haven: Yale University Press.

Greenwood, Michael J. 1975. "Research on Internal Migration in the United States: A Survey." *Journal of Economic Literature* 13:397–433.

Griffen, Clyde, and Sally Griffen. 1978. *Natives and Newcomers: The Ordering of Opportunities in Mid-Nineteenth Century Poughkeepsie.* Cambridge, Mass.: Harvard University Press.

Hamilton, Horace C. 1964. "The Negro Leaves the South." *Demography* 1:273–95.

Hansen, Niles M. 1969. "Urban Alternatives to Rural Poverty." Paper presented at the annual spring meeting of the Industrial Relations Research Association, Des Moines, Iowa.

Hanson, Robert C., and Ozzie G. Simmons. 1968. "Role Path: A Concept and Procedure for Studying Urban Communities." *Human Organization* 27:152–58.

Hartman, Edward C. 1967. *A History of American Migration.* Chicago: Rand McNally Co.

Hartz, Louis. 1955. *The Liberal Tradition in America.* New York: Harcourt, Brace.

Hathaway, Dale E. 1960. "Migration from Agriculture: The Historical Record and Its Meaning." *American Economic Review* 50:379–91.

Hauser, Philip A. 1981. "The Census of 1980." *Scientific American* 245(no.5):53–61.

Hauser, Philip M., and Otis Dudley Duncan. 1959. *The Study of Population: An Inventory and Appraisal.* Chicago: University of Chicago Press.

Hauser, Robert M. 1970. "Context and Consex: A Cautionary Tale." *American Journal of Sociology* 75:645–64.

————. 1974. "Contextual Analysis Revisited." *Sociological Methods and Research* 2:365–75.

Hays, Samuel P. 1957. *The Response to Industrialism, 1885–1914.* Chicago: University of Chicago Press.

Hess, Robert D., and Judith V. Torney. 1967. *The Development of Political Attitudes in Children.* Chicago: Aldine Publishing Co.

Hirschberg, David. 1968. "The Impact of Geographical Mobility on the Appalachian Region, 1957–1963." M.A. thesis, New York University.

Hobbs, Albert H. 1942. "Specificity and Selective Migration." *American Sociological Review* 7:772–81.

Hodge, Robert W., and Donald J. Treiman. 1966. "Occupational Mobility and Attitudes toward Negroes." *American Sociological Review* 31:93–102.

Huckshorn, Robert J. 1980. "The Role Orientations of State Party Chairmen." In *The Party Symbol*, edited by William Crotty, pp. 50–62. San Francisco: W. H. Freeman.

Hutchinson, G. E. 1944. "Limnological Studies on Connecticut. VII. A Critical Examination of the supposed Relationship between Phytoplankton Periodicity and Chemical Changes in Lake Waters." *Ecology* 25:3–61.

Hyman, Herbert H. 1959. *Political Socialization: A Study in the Psychology of Political Behavior.* Glencoe, Ill.: Free Press.

Isard, Walter. 1960. *Methods of Regional Analysis.* Cambridge, Mass.: MIT Press.

Jackman, Mary R. 1972. "Social Mobility and the Attitude toward the Political System." *Social Forces* 50:462–72.

Jackson, J. H., ed. 1969. *Migration.* Cambridge: Cambridge University Press.

Jacobson, Gary C., and Samuel Kernell. 1981. *Strategy and Choice in Congressional Elections.* New Haven: Yale University Press.

Jennings, M. Kent, and Richard G. Niemi. 1974. *The Political Character of Adolescence*. Princeton: Princeton University Press.

————. 1981. *Generations and Politics*. Princeton: Princeton University Press.

Jewell, Malcolm E., and David Olson. 1978. *American State Political Parties and Elections*. Homewood, Ill.: Dorsey Press.

Katz, Daniel, and Samuel J. Eldersveld. 1961. "The Impact of Local Party Activity upon the Electorate." *Public Opinion Quarterly* 25:1–24.

Katz, Elihu, and Paul F. Lazarsfeld. 1955. *Personal Influence*. New York: Free Press.

Katznelson, Ira. 1976. *Black Men, White Cities*. Chicago: The University of Chicago Press.

Key, V. O., Jr. 1949. *Southern Politics in State and Nation*. New York: Vintage Books.

Key, V. O. Jr., and Frank Munger. 1959. "Social Determinants and Electoral Decision: The Case of Indiana." In *American Voting Behavior*, edited by Eugene Burdick and Arthur J. Broadbeck, pp. 281–99. New York: Free Press.

Kiewiet, D. Roderick. 1983. *Macroeconomics and Micropolitics*. Chicago: University of Chicago Press.

Kish, Leslie. 1961. "A Measurement of Homogeneity in Areal Units." *Bulletin de L'Institut de Statistique*. Paris: L'Institut de Statistique, 1961.

Klapper, Joseph T. 1960. *The Effects of Mass Communication*. New York: Free Press.

Knittle, Walter A. 1936. *Early Eighteenth Century Palatine Emigration*. Philadelphia: University of Pennsylvania Press.

Kramer, Gerald H. 1970. "The Effects of Precinct-Level Canvassing on Voter Behavior." *Public Opinion Quarterly* 34:560–72.

————. 1971. "Short-term Fluctuations in U.S. Voting Behavior, 1896–1964." *American Political Science Review* 65: 131–43.

————. 1983. "The Ecological Fallacy Revisited: Aggregate versus Individual-Level Findings on Economics and Elections and Sociotropic Voting." *American Political Science Review* 77:92–111.

Krehbiel, Keith, and John R. Wright. 1983. "The Incumbency Effect in Congressional Elections: A Test of Two Explanations." *American Journal of Political Science* 27:140–57.

Kutznets, Simon. 1958. "Long Swings in the Growth of Population and in Related Economic Variables." *Proceedings of the American Philosophical Society* 102:25–52.

————. 1961. *Capital and the American Economy: Its Formation and Financing*. Princeton: Princeton University Press.

————, ed. 1957. *Population and Economic Growth: United States, 1870–1950*. Vol. 1. Philadelphia: American Philosophical Association.

Laczko, Leslie. N.d. "Contextual Analysis: The Implications for Macrosociological Research." Unpublished paper, University of Ottawa.

Ladinsky, Jack. 1967. "Sources of Geographical Mobility Among Professional Workers: A Multivariate Analysis." *Demography* 4:293–309.

Lansing, John B., and James Morgan. 1967. "The Effect of Geographical Mobility on Income." *Journal of Human Resources* 2:449–60.

Lansing, John B., and Eva Mueller. 1967. *The Geographic Mobility of Labor*. Ann Arbor, Mich.: Survey Research Center.

Lazarsfeld, Paul F., Bernard Berelson, and Hazel Gaudet. 1948. *The People's Choice*. 2d ed. New York: Columbia University Press.

Leslie, Gerald, and Arthur H. Richardson, 1961. "Lifecycle Career Patterns and the Decision to Move." *American Sociological Review* 26:894–902.

Levin, Martin L. 1961. "Social Climates and Political Socialization." *Public Opinion Quarterly* 25:596–606.

Lewin, Leif, Bo Jansson, and Dag Sorbom. 1972. *The Swedish Electorate, 1887–1968*. Uppsala: Almquist and Wiksells Boktryckeri AB.

Lieberson, Stanley. 1980. *A Piece of the Pie: Black and White Immigrants Since 1880*. Berkeley: University of California Press.

Likens, Thomas W., and C. W. Kohfeld. 1980. "Models of Massed Compliance: Contextual or Economic Approach?" Paper presented at the annual meeting of the American Political Science Association, Washington, D.C.

Lipset, Seymour M., and Stein Rokkan. 1967. "Cleavage Structures, Party Systems, and Voter Alignments: An Introduction." In *Party Systems and Voter Alignments*, edited by Seymour M. Lipset and Stein Rokkan, pp. 1–64. New York: Free Press.

Maccoby, Eleanor E. 1968. "The Development of Moral Values and Behavior in Childhood." In *Socialization and Society*, edited by John A. Clausen, pp. 229–69. Boston: Little, Brown and Co.

McGuire, William J. 1969. "The Nature of Attitudes and Attitude Change." In vol. 3 of *Handbook of Social Psychology*, 2d ed., edited by Gardner Lindzey and Elliot Aronson, pp. 136–314. Reading: Addison-Wesley.

McPhee, William N. 1963. *Formal Theories of Mass Behavior*. London: Collier-Macmillan; Free Press.

Markus, Gregory. 1982. "Political Attitudes during an Election Year: A Report on the 1980 NES Panel Study." *American Political Science Review* 76:538–69.

Marsh, Robert E. 1967. "Negro-White Differences in Geographic Mobility." *Social Security Bulletin* 30:8–19.

Martin, F. M. 1952. "Social Status and Electoral Choice in Two Constituencies." *British Journal of Sociology* 3:231–41.

Marvick, Dwaine. 1965. "The Political Socialization of the American Negro." *American Academy of Political and Social Science* 361: 112–27.

Mathews, Donald R., and James W. Prothro. 1966. *Negroes and the New Southern Politics*. New York: Harcourt, Brace and World.

May, Robert M. 1974. *Stability and Complexity in Model Ecosystems*. 2d ed. Princeton: Princeton University Press.

————, ed. 1976. *Theoretical Ecology: Principles and Applications*. Oxford: Blackwell Scientific Publications.

Mayer, P. 1968. "Migrancy and the Study of Africans in Towns." In *Readings in Urban Sociology*, edited by R. E. Pahl, New York: Pergamon Press.

Mayhew, David R. 1974. *The Electoral Connection*. New Haven: Yale University Press.

Mazie, Sara Mills, ed. 1972. *Population, Distribution, and Policy*. Vol. 5. Washington, D. C.: Government Printing Office.

Mendras, Henri. 1967. *La Fin des Paysans*. Paris: SEDEIS.

Merk, Frederick. 1978. *History of the Westward Movement*. New York: Alfred A. Knopf.

Middleton, Russell, and Snell Putney. 1963. "Student Rebellion Against Parental Political Beliefs." *Social Forces* 41:377–83.

Miller, Arthur H. 1979. "Normal Vote Analysis: Sensitivity to Change over Time." *American Journal of Political Science* 23:406–23.

Miller, Warren E. 1956. "One-Party Politics and the Voter." *American Political Science Review* 50:707–25.

Miller, Warren E., and Merrill Shanks. 1982. "Policy Directions and Presidential Leadership: Alternative Interpretations of the 1980 Presidential Election." *British Journal of Political Science* 12:299–356.

Miller, Warren E., and Philip Stouthard. 1974. "Confessional Attachment and Electoral Behavior, the Netherlands, 1972." Unpublished paper, University of Michigan.

Miller, William L. 1980. "Social Class and Party Choice in England: A New Analysis." *British Journal of Political Science* 8:257–84.

Morrison, Peter A., and Judith P. Wheeler. 1978. "The Image of 'Elsewhere' in the American Tradition of Migration." In *Human Migration: Patterns and Policies*, edited by William McNeill and R. S. Adams, pp. 75–84. Bloomington: Indiana University Press.

Newcomb, Theodore M. 1943. *Personality and Social Change*. New York: Holt.

Newcomb, Theodore M., K. E. Koenig, R. Flacks, and D. P. Warwick. 1967. *Persistence and Change: Bennington College and Its Students after 25 Years*. New York: John Wiley.

Nie, Norman H., Sidney Verba, and John R. Petrocik. 1979. *The Changing American Voter*. Rev. ed. Cambridge, Mass.: Harvard University Press.

Olsson, G. 1965. "Distance and Human Interaction: A Review and Bibliography." Bibliography Series no. 2. Philadelphia: Regional Research Institute.

Ordeshook, Peter C. 1981. "Political Disequilibrium and Scientific Inquiry." *American Political Science Review* 74:447–50.

Patterson, Thomas E. 1980. *The Mass Media Education: How Americans Choose Their President*. New York: Praeger.

Patterson, Thomas E., and Robert D. McClure. 1976. *The Unseeing Eye: The Myth of Television Power in National Elections*. New York: G. P. Putnam's Sons.

Petrocik, John R. 1980. *Party Coalitions: Realignments and the Decline of the New Deal Party System*. Chicago: University of Chicago Press.

———. N.d. "Electoral Mobilization and Party System Change: A Macrosociological Perspective." Unpublished paper, University of California at Los Angeles.

Piore, Michael J. 1968. "Negro Workers in the Mississippi Delta: Problems of Displacement and Adjustment." Paper presented at the annual winter meeting of the Industrial Relations Research Association, Madison, Wis.

Plamenatz, John. 1958. *The English Utilitarians*. 2d rev. ed. Oxford: Basil Blackwell.

Pooley, William V. 1908. *Settlement in Illinois, 1830–1850*. Madison: University of Wisconsin Press.

Price, Daniel O. 1948. "Distance and Direction as Vectors of Internal Migration, 1935–1940." *Social Forces* 27:48–53.

Prucha, Francis P. 1953. *Broadax and Bayonet: The Role of the United States Army in the Development of the Northwest, 1815–1860*. Madison: Wisconsin State Historical Society.

Prysby, Charles L. 1976. "Community Partisanship and Individual Voting

Behavior: Methodological Problems of Contextual Analysis." *Political Methodology* 1:27–61.

Przeworksi, Adam, and Glaucio A. D. Soares. 1971. "Theories in Search of a Curve: A Contextual Analysis of Left Vote." *American Political Science Review* 65:51–68.

Putnam, Robert D. 1966. "Political Attitudes and the Local Community." *American Political Science Review* 60:640–54.

Rae, Douglas. 1981. "An Altimeter for Mr. Escher's Stairway." *American Political Science Review* 74:447–55.

Rakove, Milton. 1975. *Don't Make No Waves—Don't Back No Losers: An Insider's Analysis of the Daley Machine.* Bloomington: Indiana University Press.

Rapoport, Anatol. 1966. *Two-Person Game Theory: The Essential Ideas.* Ann Arbor: University of Michigan Press.

Riker, William H. 1981. "Implications from the Disequilibrium of Majority Rule for the Study of Institutions." *American Political Science Review* 74:432–46.

Robinson, John P. 1976. "Interpersonal Influence in Election Campaigns: Two-Step Flow Hypotheses." *Public Opinion Quarterly* 40:304–19.

Särlvik, Bo. 1974. "The Social Basis of the Parties in a Developmental Perspective." In *Electoral Behavior: A Comparative Perspective*, edited by Richard Rose, pp. 371–434. New York: Free Press.

Schwarzweller, Harry K., and James S. Brown. 1967. "Social Class Origins, Rural-Urban Migration and Economic Life Chances: A Case Study." *Rural Sociology* 32:5–19.

Searing, Donald, Gerald Wright, and George Rabinowitz. 1974. "The Primacy Principle: Attitude Change and Political Socialization." Manuscript, University of North Carolina, Chapel Hill.

Sears, David O. 1968. "The Paradox of De Facto Selective Exposure without Preference for Supportive Information." In *Theories of Cognitive Consistency: A Sourcebook*, edited by Robert P. Abelson et. al., pp. 777–87. Chicago: Rand McNally.

———. 1975. "Political Socialization." In vol. 3 of *Handbook of Political Science: Theoretical Aspects of Micropolitics*, edited by F. I. Greenstein and N. W. Polsby, pp. 93–153. Reading: Addison-Wesley.

Sears, David O., and Steven H. Chaffee. 1979. "Uses and Effects of the 1976 Debates: An Overview of Empirical Studies." In *The Great Debates: Carter vs. Ford, 1976*, edited by Sidney Kraus, pp. 223–61. Bloomington: Indiana University Press.

Sears, David O., and Richard R. Lau. 1983. "Inducing Apparently Self-Interested Political Preferences." *American Journal of Political Science* 27:223–52.

Sears, David O., and John B. McConahay. 1973. *The Politics of Violence: The New Urban Blacks and the Watts Riot.* Boston: Houghton Mifflin.

Sears, David O., Richard R. Lau, Thomas R. Tyler, and Harris M. Allen, Jr. 1980. "Self-Interest vs. Symbolic Politics in Policy Attitudes and Presidential Voting." *American Political Science Review* 74:670–84.

Sell, Ralph R. 1983. "Analyzing Migration Decisions: The First Step—Whose Decisions?" *Demography* 20:299–311.

Shannon, Fred A. 1945. "A Post-Mortem on the Labor-Safety-Valve Theory." *Agricultural History* 19:31–7.

Shannon, Lyle W. 1961. "The Assimilation and Acculturation of Migrants to

Urban Areas." Madison, Wis.: Urban Program.

Shils, Edward A., and Morris Janowitz. 1948. "Cohesion and Disintegration in the Wehrmacht in World War II." *Public Opinion Quarterly* 12:280–315.

Shotwell, Louisa R. 1961. *The Harvesters: The Story of the Migrant People.* New York: Doubleday and Co.

Shryock, Henry S., Jr. 1964. *Population and Mobility within the United States.* Chicago: Community and Family Study Center, University of Chicago.

Smith, Page. 1980. *The Shaping of America: A People's History of the Young Republic.* New York: McGraw-Hill.

Sprague, John. 1973. "Three Applications of Contextual Theses: Cross Section, across Time, and across Parameters." Unpublished paper, Washington University, St. Louis, Mo.

———. 1976. "Estimating a Boudon Type Contextual Model: Some Practical and Theoretical Problems of Measurement." *Political Methodology* 3:333–54.

Sprague, John, and Louis P. Westefield. 1979a. "Contextual Effects from Behavioral Contagion." Paper presented at the annual meeting of the Western Political Science Association, Portland, Oreg.

———. 1979b. "An Interpretive Reconstruction of Some Aggregate Models of Contextual Effects." Paper presented at the annual meeting of the Southern Political Science Association, Gatlinburg, Tenn.

Sternlieb, George, and James W. Hughes. 1980. "The Changing Demography of the Central City." *Scientific American* 243(no. 2):48–53.

Stinchcombe, Arthur L. 1975. "Social Structure and Politics." In *Handbook of Political Science*, vol. 3, *Macropolitical Theory*, edited by Fred I. Greenstein and Nelson W. Polsby, pp. 557–622. Reading, Mass.: Addison-Wesley.

Stipak, Brian, and Carl Hensler. 1982. "Statistical Inference in Contextual Analysis." *American Journal of Political Science* 26:151–75.

Stouffer, Samuel A. 1940. "Intervening Opportunities: A Theory Relating Mobility and Distance." *American Sociological Review* 5:845–67.

———. 1955. *Communism, Conformity and Civil Liberties.* New York: Doubleday and Co.

Strodtbeck, Fred L. 1941. "A Contribution to the Method of Intervening Opportunity Analysis." *American Sociological Review* 14:490–97.

———. 1950. "Population, Distance and Migration from Kentucky." *Sociometry* 13:123–30.

Sullivan, John L., James E. Piereson, and George E. Marcus. 1978. "Ideological Constraint in the Mass Public: A Methodological Critique and Some New Findings." *American Journal of Political Science* 22:233–49.

Suval, Elizabeth M., and Horace C. Hamilton. 1965. "Some New Evidence on Educational Selectivity in Migration to and from the South." *Social Forces* 43:536–47.

Switzer, Robert E. 1961. "The Effects of Family Moves on Children." *Mental Hygiene* 45:528–36.

Taeuber, Karl E., Leonard Chiazze, Jr., and William Haenszel. 1968. *Migration in the United States: An Analysis of Residence Histories.* Public Health Monograph no. 77. Washington, D.C.: Government Printing Office.

Taeuber, Conrad, and Irene B. Taeuber. 1958. *The Changing Population of the United States.* New York: John Wiley.

Taeuber, Irene B. 1972. "The Changing Distribution of the Population of the United States in the Twentieth Century." In vol. 5 of *Population, Distribu-*

tion and Policy, edited by Sara Mills Mazie, pp. 29–107. Washington, D.C.: U.S. Commission on Population Growth and the American Future.

Tannenbaum, Arnold S., and Jerald G. Backman. 1964. "Structural versus Individual Effects." *American Journal of Sociology* 69:585–95.

Taylor, Peter J., and R. J. Johnston. 1979. *Geography of Elections*. New York: Holmes and Meier Publishers.

Theil, Henri. 1971. *Principles of Econometrics*. New York: John Wiley.

Thernstrom, Stephen. 1964. *The Other Bostonians: Poverty and Progress in the American Metropolis 1880–1970*. Cambridge, Mass.: Harvard University Press.

Thomas, Robert N., and John M. Hunter. 1980. *Internal Migration Systems in the Developing World*. Boston: Schenkman Publishing Co.

Thomassen, Jacques. 1976. "Party Identification as a Cross-National Concept: Its Meaning in the Netherlands." In *Party Identification and Beyond: Representations of Voting and Party Competition*, edited by Ian Budge, Ivor Crew, and Dennis Farlie, pp. 63–77. London: John Wiley.

Thornbrough, E. L. 1961. "Segregation in Indiana during the Klan Era of the 1920s." *Mississippi Historical Review* 84:1401–23.

Tilly, Charles. 1967. "Race and Migration to the American City." In *The Metropolitan Enigma: Inquiries into the Nature and Dimensions of America's Urban Crisis*, edited by James Q. Wilson, pp. 124–46. Washington D.C.: U.S. Chamber of Commerce.

Tingsten, Herbert. 1937. *Political Behavior: Studies in Election Statistics*. London: P. S. King.

Todaro, M. J. 1969. "A Model of Labor Migration and Urban Unemployment in Less Developed Countries." *American Economic Review* 59:138–41.

U.S. Bureau of the Census. 1966. Reasons for Moving: March 1962 to March 1963. *Current Population Reports*, ser. P-20, no. 154. Washington, D.C., 22 August.

———. 1971. Mobility of the Population of the United States: March 1969 to March 1970. *Current Population Reports*, ser. P-20, no. 210. Washington, D.C., 15 January.

———. 1983. Geographical Mobility: March 1980 to March 1981. *Current Population Reports*, ser. P-20, no. 377. Washington, D.C., January.

Valen, Henry, and Daniel Katz. 1964. *Political Parties in Norway*. London: Tavistock.

Verba, Sidney, and Norman H. Nie. 1972. *Participation in America: Political Democracy and Social Equality*. New York: Harper and Row.

von Kaufmann, Franz-Xavier, ed. 1975. *Bevolkerungsbewegung zwischen Quantität und Qualität*. Stuttgart: Enke.

Wattenberg, Martin P. 1984. *The Decline of Political Parties in the United States, 1952–1980*. Cambridge, Mass.: Harvard University Press.

Wilson, James Q. 1962. *The Amateur Democrat: Club Politics in Three Cities*. Chicago: University of Chicago Press.

Wirth, Louis. 1938. "Urbanism as a Way of Life." *American Journal of Sociology* 44:3–24.

Wolfinger, Raymond E., and Stephen Rosenstone. 1980. *Who Votes?* New Haven: Yale University Press.

Wolpert, Julian. 1966. "Migration as an Adjustment to an Environmental Stress." *Journal of Social Issues* 22:91–102.

———. 1967. "Distance and Directional Bias in Inter-Urban Migratory

Streams." *Annals of the Association of American Geographers* 57:677–86.

Woodward, C. Vann. 1967. *The Strange Career of Jim Crow*. New York: Oxford University Press.

Wright, Gerald C., Jr. 1977. "Contextual Models of Electoral Behavior: The Southern Wallace Vote." *American Political Science Review* 71:495–508.

Wyckoff, Mikel. 1980. "Belief System Constraint and Policy Voting: A Test of the Unidimensional Consistency Model." *Political Behavior* 2:115–46.

Zachariah, K. C., and Julien Conde. 1981. *Migration in West Africa*. New York: Oxford University Press.

Zipf, George K. 1946. "The P P/D Hypothesis: On the Intercity Movement of Persons." *American Sociological Review* 11:677–86.

Zuiches, James. 1981. "Residential Preferences in the United States." In *Nonmetropolitan America in Transition*, edited by Amos H. Hawley and Sara Mills Mazie, pp. 72–115. Chapel Hill: University of North Carolina Press.

Index